The Monologue

The Monologue

✦

From Mystery to Mastery

With 50 Original Monologues

By Peter DeAnello

iUniverse, Inc.

New York Lincoln Shanghai

The Monologue
From Mystery to Mastery

iUniverse, Inc.

For information address:
iUniverse, Inc.
2021 Pine Lake Road, Suite 100
Lincoln, NE 68512
www.iuniverse.com

ISBN: 0-595-30918-6

Printed in the United States of America

Contents

The easy to follow process of authoring your own career-launching monologues.

SPECIAL THANKS

First, to my wife, Kaye, who continues to encourage me through every endeavor. She is my greatest support, partner and best friend in life.

To my children, who are my reason for all that I do.

To my extended families, who have always cheered me on through each failure as well as each success.

To Dan Lauria for all the years of example, mentoring and support.

To Rick Ramage for his unconditional friendship, mentoring and for being a wonderful example that if the dream (as well as the talent) is realized, then hard, focused work through early mornings and late nights won't matter.

To Steve Klayman for his friendship, patience and belief that someday I would understand the importance of structure in writing.

To Paul Rohrer for his trust, support, editing and partnership.

To Richard and Roe Glasser, for years of loyalty and support in my talents.

To Alan Shackelford & Ellen Ranson for their talent and support in helping to edit this book.

To the actors and my staff at Big Fish Talent and the Write To Act Workshops for their dreams, creativity and trust. Together, we'll prove that encouragement and hard work changes lives.

INTRODUCTION

If you:

1) have been frustrated with finding *dynamic* audition material

2) have heard or believed that monologues are passé

3) have never fully understood what makes a great monologue

4) question the importance of the monologue as one of the greatest tools in building professional acting careers

5) are curious in any way about how to easily write your own monologue

then you owe it to yourself (and your talent) to read *The Monologue, from Mystery to Mastery* and implement the six clearly defined and easily understood steps to finding or writing your own successful monologues.

Why is it so important for every actor to possess at least one great monologue? Because it is very likely that:

There will come a day in every actor's career when the use of, or lack of, a great monologue will seriously affect the success of that actor. That will be a defining moment in the actor's career. It's a matter of career choice; a matter of asset vs. liability.

Let's make this point easily understood. The monologue is an *asset* (or a *dynamic* piece) when it creates a favorable impression or an acting opportunity either for the present or future. It's a *liability* when it creates an unfavorable impression that may also last a lifetime.

The monologue won't allow you to hide. It's you, your talent and the truth of the character. That's why many successful actors embrace monologues and many unsuccessful actors flee from them. That is also why:

The successful actor is the actor who is always in search of finding or writing that audition piece (monologue) that is *in equal collaboration with* his or her talent.

With that in mind, I have spent years studying and perfecting the structure, construction and use of the monologue.

Now it's time for every actor to fully understand and appreciate the power of this simple, yet critical vehicle for building a successful career.

Here's a silly, but poignant analogy:

Walking into any audition without the best fully prepared audition material is like a carpenter trying to build a house with a plastic hammer.

No one wants to hire a carpenter who doesn't possess the best skills, *with* tools to match. Any technician may possess the greatest skills, but without the proper tools to work with, that person can't fully prove his or her worth as a technician or artisan.

This book will also confront some old beliefs and misinformation concerning the monologue and its usefulness (the monologue is probably the most misunderstood and misused of all acting tools). You will finish with the information necessary to further take charge of your career.

However, remember that information is not power, *applied* information is power.

So, when the right information is applied to persistent and consistent dedication, *magic happens!*

The following are just some of the reasons the monologue is an important tool for the serious actor:

1) The Extra Yard

As with anything else, some auditioners favor the monologue and some don't.

It won't always be asked for, or required, but it may mean the difference between being cast in a role one day or losing it to the actor who is willing to perform one…who is *prepared to go that extra yard.*

2) Comfort level

The monologue is one of the best measures for an actor's self confidence, talent and level of experience in front of an audience or camera. There's an unmistakable and captive confidence that shines through with preparedness.

3) Seizing the Moment

I love the actor who, after a scripted audition, offers a monologue. I almost always make time for that actor. I feel it is a demonstration of aptitude, a confident attitude and preparedness.

Many auditioners may refuse to see it because of time restraints; however, subliminally, the actor leaves them with an assurance of preparedness and professionalism. This also presents the monologue as a tremendous psychological (as well as physical) tool in the audition process.

Can an actor be over-prepared?

Les Brown once said, "It's better to be prepared for an opportunity and not have one, than to have an opportunity and not be prepared."

4) Work Ethic

Master the monologue and you master an important step in discipline as an actor. If you won't spend the hours needed to produce a captivating and believable two to three minute monologue, how can I trust that you'll be disciplined enough to spend hours, days, or even weeks working together to develop a character?

PREPAREDNESS IN SEARCH FOR OPPORTUNITY

As an independent contractor, it's up to you to create new opportunities for your talent through smart preparedness.

As an actor, I searched for one book that would explain the ABC's to finding or writing that special piece that would capture an audience and truly showcase my talent. I've spent years talking with very talented actors about their processes and attending workshops. Add to that the thousands of auditions I've sat through, then the years of working with actors to develop this process. That has all culminated in creating the simplest and most concise process for finding or developing the ultimate monologue.

The bottom line is *preparedness in search for opportunity.* That is how I encourage you to view your career from this day on.

START BY APPROACHING YOUR CAREER FIRST AS A BUSINESS

In almost every acting workshop I coach, I ask this question, "How many actors in this room are business owners?" If every actor's hand is not raised, I ask the question again and again until every hand goes up. You are an independent contractor in a business about you. It's a fickle business that doesn't believe it needs you, but can't wait until you walk in and deliver the perfect audition.

As *the business of you*, you need to present proof that you can and will deliver when your employer asks for a product. Your picture and resume are important, but when the rubber meets the road, it's all about you and your talent.

SO, MAKE AN ACTIVE DECISION TOWARDS CHANGING A HABIT

Good habits=Smart preparedness

Isn't it true in any career, art, sport, and hobby, that dedication and commitment to achieving your goal is only half the battle?

If your approach to success is through bad habit or incomplete instruction, you'll never fully realize your dream.

The older I get, the harder I find it is to change or develop new habits. However, just because I've spent years developing a habit, it doesn't mean the habit is a healthy or prosperous one. It may mean that I've simply reached a comfort level…or avoided one.

I used to avoid sit-ups, until I made an *active decision* not to. *Bingo! As* with anything else, it's a *decision* to hide from the monologue in fear or embrace it as an ally. In any learning experience, when information is low, fear is high. Likewise, when information is high, fear diminishes.

How would you feel if you went to your first day of work, in a very technical career, and your boss said, "Just get started," with no direction? You would be lost, right? Yet, many actors' choose to *wing it* in their approach to finding or creating a calling card for their talent.

Believe it or not, acting is a very technical profession. *Winging it* isn't a good way to establish and maintain a career.

In all my years in this business, from actor to writer to agent to producer, sitting through thousands of monologues, six very important steps have stood out over and over again, either in application or neglect. These are the steps that create a successful monologue.

This book is divided into three areas of concentration:

1) I will present the problems, solutions and successful tips for monologues and auditions. I feel it is necessary to understand and explain the proper use, time and necessity for this tool.

2) Presented are 50 original monologues, rated according to the Six Step Process. Not all will meet each step, on purpose.

3) We will discuss in simple detail, with example, how to write your own monologue according to the Six Step Process.

I suggest that you read this book twice. First, to understand the steps I will speak of and to allow me to answer the tough questions. The second time you read through, use this as a workbook to seek out and find, or to write your signature monologues.

Let's begin!

1

Answers and Explanations

Why start here? Because when I have your trust, I have your full attention.

You might say, "Who is this guy, and why should I listen to or believe him?"

That's fair for anything in life, when you're in search for answers or for trust in any product or person.

Again, if your fear is high, that means your information is low. When you have the information and your questions or concerns answered, the fear diminishes.

So, let's confront the most frequent concerns about monologues and with the auditioning process. After that, I'll present the Six Step Process.

1) WHY IS IT SO IMPORTANT FOR AN ACTOR TO HAVE GOOD AMMUNITION?

Good actors many times sabotage themselves with incomplete or bad monologues. That's like going to a corporate job interview in ripped jeans, sneakers and a stained tee shirt.

Here's something most actors, unfortunately, don't see from the other side of the desk. You don't see it because it's a totally subconscious situation.

I've seen so many talented actors choose a monologue that they wrestle with to make better than it is. As I watch, I find myself thinking, "I know this person is a better actor than this."

In many cases, it's the material actors choose to audition with (not their acting talent) that holds them back.

Many auditions fall short because the actor is at a level of competence so far above the piece of work they have chosen to audition with.

So, what we witness is a competent actor working hard to lift the level of writing to their level of acting…Thus, we really don't have a good sense of the true level of acting talent being reviewed. That leaves a question in the minds of the auditioners of how good a talent really is.

Here's another point to consider:

If the auditioner doesn't know your work and is already interested in another actor from past experience, you can't afford to leave the slightest question in that auditioner's mind when you leave.

You need to *own* that role in the auditioner's mind as well as your own.

2) THE WRITING

It has to start here. Every successful audition, monologue, play, or screenplay has to begin with the writing.

The actor who believes he/she can compensate for unfinished or bad writing is sadly on a downward spiral from the beginning.

As long as I live, I'll never be able to drive this point home often enough.

If a house painter doesn't first scrape off the chipping paint on a house, it doesn't matter how many coats he applies over it; the mistakes are still blatantly in the preparation of the work.

You can't turn bad writing into good writing.

No matter how good an actor is, bad or incomplete writing is just that. If the actor's talent exists at a higher level than the writing talent in the monologue, what that actor spends the next several minutes doing is reaching down to pull the writer up to his/her level of acting ability.

When both the writer and the actor are performing at the top of their game, magic happens. It's not your responsibility to make the writer look better than he or she is, and vice versa.

It's a *collaborative* effort. It must be.

3) THE COLLABORATIVE EFFORT

The very career of acting is part of a collaborative effort that begins with the writer and ends with the director.

Remember this in both the creative and business aspects of your chosen profession,

Not dependence, not independence...Inter-dependence!

You are on a collaborative journey with the writer or with the writing of the piece. When both the level of the writing and the level of the actor's talent start on an equally high level of competence, the result is creatively rewarding.

Consider the writer and the monologue your partners.

4) MONOLOGUES ARE PASSE AND OUTDATED! NOBODY ASKS FOR THEM ANYMORE

I own an on-camera talent agency. I won't consider anyone for the agency who doesn't have a monologue. I ask for that first. If someone doesn't have one, I ask that actor to come back when ready.

I believe the monologue is as important to an actor as a hammer is to a carpenter.

Could you imagine hiring a carpenter, then having him show up without his tools? How much faith would you have in his work now?

The reason I love the monologue is because all the responsibility is on the actor to create the character and the emotion.

As a talent representative, if you can't hold my attention, I know you're not ready to hold the attention of my clients.

If you're not successful with a monologue, I frankly don't need to see a commercial read (which is what I do next in most auditions, hand the actor a commercial script and ask them to come back in five minutes and read). If you can't hold my attention on something you should have prepared, what makes me think you can do it for something more spontaneous?

I was auditioning CoCo, a young actress. (I believe she was seventeen years old at the time).

When I asked for a monologue, she presented me with a sheet of paper with the titles of 21 monologues listed, and humbly suggested that she would be happy to do any one or all of them at my request.

I was impressed, surprised and curious at the same time. I asked about the titles I didn't recognize (at least half of them) and she nervously responded, "I wrote those." I asked for a few of those first. They were wonderful!

All together, I think I asked her to do six that I chose randomly. She was memorized, connected and wonderfully talented. Do you think I needed to see anything else?

Quite frankly, I was quietly cheering for her the moment CoCo handed me the sheet of paper. I knew I would represent her after the first few seconds of the first piece.

I just enjoyed the audition so much that I asked her to continue. I still represent that young lady today and I'm confident she will go very far in her career.

CoCo didn't rely on her beauty to make the strongest impression in the audition (she's a very beautiful young lady). It was her preparedness and her talent that sold me on representation.

Now, as to who asks for monologues anymore, consider once again the psychology behind offering one. Let's say that no one ever asks for a monologue in your auditions, but you're prepared and offer one in the appropriate situations. Appropriate excludes most commercial and industrial auditions.

Let's say you audition quite often for theatre, series television, or film. You do a good job with the material they give you. However, you have a monologue similar to the character they are auditioning.

You suggest, "I have a monologue prepared that is similar to that character. Would you like to see it?"

Even if they decline, due to time constraints, you leave them with a very positive impression. They will remember you (if not for this project, for another), I promise you.

Conversely, if someone asks for a monologue (and I always do), and you don't have anything prepared, what does that say? It tells me the actor is not fully prepared for every possible audition situation.

5) BUT I'M JUST NOT A GOOD AUDITIONER

Learn to become one. It's part of the business of acting that every actor needs to develop a proficiency for. If you were hired to be a receptionist, I wouldn't advise that you tell your prospective boss during the interview, "I'm just not good at answering the phone." Or, if you are applying for a position in a wait staff that you offer, "I'm just not good at working on my feet for that amount of time."

There's a four-letter word that follows for people who tell me that in an audition...*NEXT!*

6) BUT I WAS INSTRUCTED NEVER TO WRITE MY OWN MONOLOGUE

Here's where I've receive the most resistance in coaching this Six Step Process. There is some resistance towards actors writing their own monologues.

The belief is that authoring an original audition piece:

- **lends an unfair advantage because the actor will face another author's writing 99% of the time, and**
- **it will not present an honest account of what an actor will do with another writer's work.**

I can appreciate the reasoning behind both valuable facts. At my alma mater, I was instructed according to the very same beliefs.

Consider that most self-authored monologues are written from life experience. That means you have an automatic emotional attachment to that piece because of the emotional attachment to memory and experience.

We are emotional beings to begin with. So, consequently, you bring what I refer to as an automatic *third dimension* to your work. You have the emotional attachment in place because the inner monologue is strong.

Add to that the artist's temperament and what usually develops is a highly cathartic, emotionally explosive, comic or dramatic piece (or at least the beginnings of one).

Now, that launches the artist immediately into the third dimension of creativity (the emotional connection to the work), or as we'll discuss, the dimension of *love*.

This means that no matter whose work you pick up next, you will no longer be satisfied with settling for two dimensions in developing that character. You will always be working harder to re-create the feeling you naturally had in your original piece.

For that reason, and for a better appreciation in the writer's attention to structure, word and action, I believe that every actor should author at least one monologue.

In my experience, the talent of the actor who struggles through authoring an audition vehicle will develop much faster than the actor who has never tried.

Why? Because of the underlying emotional understanding and expression that is automatically attached to any life experience, whether painful or comical. This is naturally conveyed in the performance when an actor is emotionally attached to the material because it is re-lived each time. That is the *inner-monologue* at its best, the dimensions of emotion that truly supports every wonderful piece of work.

The self-written work is the springboard for the young actor to begin good work habits, while developing a clear understanding of that third dimension of character.

During my acting days, I searched voraciously for the perfect monologue, the best proving measure of my talent. I searched through monologue books, newspapers, court testimonials, plays, screenplays, and even questioned random people on the street about their life-altering experiences. It wasn't until I was encouraged to pen my own monologue, during an acting apprenticeship at Actors Theatre of Louisville (Kentucky), that I realized how I had been limiting my approach to my talent.

So, ultimately, I'm encouraging you to have a healthy balance of classics, contemporary and self-authored pieces in your repertoire.

In my experience in Los Angeles and New York (whether in front of the camera or behind), when an actor performs an original piece well, the auditioners are always impressed. I was never reprimanded or looked down upon for having a self-authored piece.

7) WRITE MY OWN MONOLOGUE? BUT I'M NOT A WRITER

Awesome! You weren't an actor before you *made the choice* to become one either.

I'm not saying you have to write if you don't want to. This process offers the Six Steps in *locating* a winning monologue, as well as the foundation for authoring your own.

8) (Does this sound familiar?) THERE'S NO TIME!

There is always a time limit to the search, i.e.; "I need this for class, or for an upcoming audition, right away."

This is not news. Let's be honest and remind ourselves that most of us made a habit out of waiting until the last minute to complete any task. Remember school?
(Cramming for tests, pulling all-nighters to hand in a report, etc.)

So, what usually happens is:

with the time constraint clearly in mind, the actor begins to negotiate…"I can compensate with my acting ability."

Advice: Drill the well *before* you need the water.

Is this what happens next?

THE SEARCH:

A) First the actor asks other actors for monologues they would recommend.

When their compadres either refuse to give up their treasures, or can't help because they're in the midst of the same searching process, the actor then:

B) searches every script and story that seems to have roles that *fit* his/her casting profile. When that proves futile,

C) the actor searches monologue books, but becomes frustrated with those also (99% never fall under even one or two of the Six Step Process. I'll explain that in detail later).

So,

D) our actor becomes really hard to live with (who wouldn't?), while bumping that spinning head against the proverbial *brick wall.*

E) Then, in total frustration, our dedicated artist spends hours in a library or bookstore reviewing all the old over-used monologues in the hope that one of them isn't *too* over-used.

F) After a session or two with a therapist, either the therapist or family member (usually a non-artist with a clearer vision through practicality) suggests that he/she write an original piece.

G) The actor usually responds with something like, "Ohmygod, they just don't understand me. I'm not a writer, I'm an actor. Besides, my college professor told me that I should never write my own monologue. They just don't understand!"

H) So, after avoiding that last great piece of advice, and weathering a few fights with a spouse or significant other, due to an acute case of *moody-mania* (caused by the fear of something new and different), our actor begins the negotiation process by engaging in an inner battle between the artist/perfectionist and the lazy house painter.

That's when our actor rises up or gives up.

9) FINE! THEN WHERE DO I FIND A GOOD MONOLOGUE OR THE IDEAS TO WRITE THEM?

A) The greatest teacher I've ever had is life experience

B) The Internet has made it so much easier to locate monologues, or to find the ammunition for a good one

C) Click on news and read current events

D) Go to a courtroom and record testimonies

E) Of course, there are theatre, film and TV scripts to sift through

F) Also consider reversing the genre on an already produced piece

A great example of this is one of my favorite monologues. It's from the film, *And Justice For All*. Al Pacino did the lead role in 1972. It's the last monologue of the film, when Pacino's character (who is defending a guilty judge) actually tells the truth about the judge and ruins his own career (Pacino's) in the process. I've always encouraged women to do that piece. It's *gender-less* and a great monologue to show strength and vulnerability.

Besides that, any man will be compared to Al Pacino if the auditioner knows the script. A woman, however, has a clean slate in the *comparison* category.

10) WHEN I LIFT A MONOLOGUE FROM A FILM OR PLAY, IT DOESN'T SEEM TO HAVE THE SAME IMPACT

This is a common problem. Many times an actor will work on a piece from a larger entity, and it doesn't translate well. Why?

Within a larger piece, the character and story have had some time to build momentum in regard to audience emotions. The monologue from *And Justice For All* occurs at the very end of the story. The characters are well developed at this point. We've already lived with them for the past two hours. The attorney begins the piece at a highly emotional place in the film. As a separate piece, the monologue cannot be started at that same intensity, or the actor won't have anywhere to build.

Every monologue is a story within itself when presented apart from the larger piece. It must be approached that way, with it's own beginning, middle and end.

11) WHAT ABOUT PIECING TOGETHER A MONOLOGUE FROM DIFFERENT SPEECHES OR CHARACTERS?

It's been done many times. However, be careful, because re-writing or making adjustments to someone else's piece is dangerous. Aside from the possibility of plagiarism, you face a problem with continuity.

A character, as well as a story, has a rhythm.

Make sure that you're not altering the emotional rhythms so much that the audience thinks, "That character wouldn't say or do that."

12) WHEN DO I PRESENT A MONOLOGUE AND HOW DO I ASK IF THE AUDITIONER WANTS TO SEE ONE?

Important: Only ask to present a monologue after you have already done a good job on the material the auditioner presents you with.

If your audition doesn't go well, you may want to leave to fight another day. If you know the auditioner well, then offering a monologue after a mediocre audition may be your saving grace.

I suggest that you offer a monologue that is nearest to the character you are auditioning for. I also suggest that you present the offer this way, "I've prepared a monologue that is very close to the character in this script. I would like to do it for you if you have time."

Remember this key phrase that I encourage each of my agency actors to write on a sticky note and attach to their bathroom mirror:

Always be hungry enough to work and humble enough to listen.

Humility and talent are always welcome and respected. Always present yourself in that way.

13) HOW MANY MONOLOGUES SHOULD I HAVE READY?

How many tools does a carpenter need to get the job done well?

As many as it takes.

The young lady I spoke about had 21 at that time. I'm sure she has many more now. Is she an over-achiever, a fanatic, or thoroughly prepared? When I studied acting, we were encouraged to have at least one contemporary comic, one contemporary dramatic and one classic monologue ready at all times. The operative words in that last sentence are *at least.*

14) WHAT TO PRESENT TO WHOM?

Again, you probably won't need a monologue for commercial or industrial auditions. I encourage you to be prepared with at least one for film and television auditions.

Have you ever said, or heard an actor say, "My agent doesn't know what I can really do." or "I keep being sent out for the same type of role. I can do more than that."

Guess what? The monologue is your best opportunity to show your agent what else you can do, the fastest way possible. Yes, you can keep doing play after play, hoping your agent will attend and appreciate your versatility over time. That takes too long. Show your agent now, and don't miss out on all those auditions you could have had.

15) HOW LONG SHOULD MY MONOLOGUES BE?

Most monologues are too long. I used to say three minutes or under. I have changed that to two minutes, whenever possible.

Your auditioner, in most cases, will know within the first minute how talented you are and if there is a role for you in a project. Leave that person wanting more, always.

16) WHAT ABOUT A MONOLOGUE SHOULD CATCH THE AUDITIONER'S ATTENTION FIRST?

Too many monologues, as in too many auditions, begin with dialogue.

Ironically, the less that is said, the better, especially at the start of the piece.

If every story, whatever the length, surrounds a character at the height of conflict, then let's see the conflict. I'm not encouraging you to cry, scream or shout. What do you generally do when wrestling with a decision or situation? Usually, you go deep within the recesses of your mind and heart to wrestle emotionally with the situation. Always start with that.

It's not so much what you say, but the inner struggle that occurs before and during the time that you *have to say it*. That is the most interesting moment of any monologue.

So, to answer the question, don't always start with the dialogue. Speak when you *have to*, not just because the curtain has risen or the director has said, "Action!"

What catches my attention first is the actor who is internally wrestling with the conflict of the piece before speaking.

This is not a *method-acting* lesson, it's the moment in time that an audience member can inwardly relate to the character, because everyone struggles with a decision or situation every day. When we recognize that in the character, we empathize and thus, we are pulled into the situation. Do that from the start and you hold our attention.

17) WHAT'S THE DIFFERENCE BETWEEN PERFORMING A MONOLOGUE FOR STAGE OR FOR SCREEN?

I'm asked this question often. Unless you are projecting to an 800-seat house, or the role calls for slapstick or immense physical prowess, there is not much difference.

Whether for stage or screen, your auditioner wants the honesty of the character within the confines of the situation.

I prefer a simple, honest read. I may ask you to do the same piece several ways to see how easily directed you can be, but always start with simple honesty.

18) I'VE HEARD THE TERM "NICHE" MONOLOGUE. WHAT IS A NICHE MONOLOGUE?

A monologue is considered *niche* when it encompasses genres such as farce, thriller, mystery or black comedy. A period piece, or one that requires a regional accent is also considered *niche*. These are specific pieces that you should have in your arsenal, but aren't considered the contemporary mainstream comic, dramatic or classical piece that most auditioners ask for.

Some examples include the street tough with a Brooklyn accent, a southern belle, a farcical character (in a role that may involve physical comedy), the class clown, the murderer, etc.

A good way to search or create one is by first reviewing story genres, such as Drama, Dramady, Situation Comedy, Black Comedy, Farce, Classics, Mystery Thriller, etc.

These are monologues that you wouldn't necessarily want to use in a general audition, but will come in very handy for specific situations.

It is so important to have an arsenal of niche pieces to pull out at any given moment, because those are the monologues that give you the *edge* in specific circumstances.

For example, you're in a casting director's office, auditioning for a role in a western series. Only after you do a good job with the script in hand, do you suggest that you have a monologue very much like the character you're auditioning for. You ask if they would like to see it. If they are interested in you for the character and have time, they may say yes.

Then you launch into your rodeo monologue, or your saloon tough guy, gunslinger, etc. Even if they don't have time to see it, but are interested in you, it may be what helps to get you the call back. You've left the impression that you are a well-prepared, professional actor. As we've discussed before, that part of it is subliminal.

A word to the wise concerning *niche* monologues:

Decide what your strengths are as a performer or consider your special skills and find or write a monologue around each strength or special skill.

For example, if you are proficient at martial arts, a magician, a singer, or a professional clown, find or create a piece that may display or suggest that specific skill.

19) ACCENTS AND REGIONAL MONOLOGUES

Unless the role you're auditioning for requires a Texas accent, a New York accent, an English accent, etc., don't use a monologue that requires one for a general audition. It will limit your *castability*.

As a young actor, I had this great Brooklyn street tough monologue and used it as my contemporary dramatic piece. After a while, I wondered why the only role I would be considered for was the street tough, when I also wanted to perform comedy, farce, etc.

One of my coaches asked, "When are you going to file that monologue in the *niche* category and find a main-stream piece?"

20) NEVER ABANDON YOUR SEARCH FOR GOOD MONOLOGUES

Keep your tools sharpened. Never stop looking for or writing good audition material. You will develop and find your winning pieces, but unless they are ageless, you will grow out of them in time.

I can no longer play that street kid anymore. It's like good resume pictures. You're going to need new ones soon.

2

Proper Audition Decorum

1) INTRODUCE THE MONOLOGUE BY CHARACTER AND TITLE. NO OTHER INFORMATION IS NEEDED

Many times actors will start the audition by explaining what's happening in the scene, or what the play is about. That's insecurity. Inwardly, the actor is saying, "This monologue is unclear and I don't want you to get lost, or you'll think it's my fault."

Create the atmosphere and be in the moment.

All we need to know is your name, the character's name, and from what larger work it was pulled from.

For example, "My name is Johnny Smith and I'll be doing Bobby, from *Fearless Existence*." Now, start the monologue. If it is a complete monologue, we won't require any other information.

Slate that information as you, the actor, not the character.

I've had actors walk into the room *in character*, or slate *in character*. Many times it's for the James Dean type role. They believe that *brooding* through the audition will make us get on the phone with their agents afterwards and say, "Send *him* back, he *is* that character." What generally happens next is we get on the phone and say, "Please don't ever send him again. No one is going to want to be on the set for twelve hours a day with that guy."

We want to see you *become* the role. When you slate, slate as you, pleasant and personable. Then, become the character and show us the transition you can easily make when asked to. That is more impressive than keeping us guessing whether you're a closet axe murderer or not.

2) DON'T ASK FOR PREP TIME FOR VOCAL OF PHYSICAL EXERCISES. JUST TAKE A DEEP BREATH AND START

We don't need to become exposed to your training, nor do we want to sit through your acting coach's warm up exercise. That isn't a sign of a serious or professional actor.

Exercises are to be done before you enter the room.

Sitting through a warm up sends one message—*actor in training.*

Nobody wants to hire the *actor in training*. They want the *professional actor*.

3) DON'T LINGER OR OVERSELL YOURSELF

I've witnessed many actors sell themselves right out of a job before or after a monologue, by lingering in the office or going through the list of credits on their resume.

Let both the monologue and resume speak for themselves. Remember, leave your auditioner wanting more.

If there's interest in you or your work, let the auditioner request that you stay.

4) NO PROPS

Props are dangerous and distracting in an audition. Too many times, the attention is diverted from the actor to the prop.

I once sat through three takes of an actor who was so nervous during a monologue that he kept trying unsuccessfully to light a cigarette. Finally, I pointed to the *no smoking* sign behind him on the office wall and thanked him for coming.

I've always been a firm believer that the actor needs to be the focal point in the audition, not a prop. They are not needed, nor are they welcome by the auditioner.

Leave hats, guns, knives, cigarettes, cigars, etc., home and act. If you absolutely have to have a prop for a monologue, choose a different monologue.

I once had a man bring his wife into the audition room with him, for no other reason than to have her to talk to during the audition. She was a prop. I was more interested in *her* acting ability after the audition, because if she didn't get cast beside him in the play, I was afraid he wouldn't know how to talk to anyone else.

A chair is the only set dressing you need, and even then *ask* if you may use it.

5) DON'T REARRANGE THE OFFICE FURNITURE

The space you are standing or sitting in is yours during an audition, not the furniture or props in the room. Don't assume you can change or re-arrange things at will.

6) STAY STILL AS MUCH AS POSSIBLE

Don't wander or jump around, and don't walk into an office and start screaming out your monologue in the name of *emoting*. All you will leave the auditioner with is the question of whether the neighbors are calling the police, concerned that someone might be getting murdered in there.

7) ASK IF THE AUDITIONERS WOULD PREFER THAT YOU PERFORM THE MONOLOGUE DIRECTLY TO THEM

Though auditioners want to be caught up in the action and emotion of your piece, most would prefer to not feel obliged to immediately respond to your work. They would rather observe without responsibility.

Some do prefer that you look them in the eyes. That is why it is absolutely acceptable for you to ask.

Most of the time, I ask actors to focus on a spot on the wall and pretend it is a camera lens. I want to make sure that, even if they are not auditioning for camera work, they can stay focused.

8) WHERE DO I FOCUS?

If the character is seated in the piece, focus eye level, but on a spot just to the side of the auditioner (assuming the auditioner is seated). If you are speaking to a character that is standing, then focus just above the auditioner and a few inches to either side (pretending the character is eye level with you).

In other words, don't make someone nine feet tall or two feet tall. Make them average height, focusing on a spot as close to the auditioner as possible.

If you are auditioning for two or more people in a room, find a spot equally between them.

If there is a camera in the room, and you are working with a reader, ask if the auditioner would prefer for you speak to the reader or the camera.

9) KEEP A SAFE AND RESPECTFUL DISTANCE AND NEVER TOUCH THE AUDITIONER

I heard a story in Hollywood once that made me very upset. An actor was auditioning with a scene that required that his character spit on another character. What do you think that actor did? He actually spit on the casting director during the audition.

I was a reader for a casting director in Hollywood in the early 1980s. They were auditioning women for a new TV series. One young lady became really involved in her role and, as the character is supposed to slap my character in the face, she slapped me. I was not ready for it and worked for the rest of the day with a red face. The producer phoned the agent while she was still in the room and demanded that the actress never be sent to his office again.

Always respect the people you are auditioning for or with. If the scene calls for a kiss, or physical action, never assume that you have that privilege.

10) DON'T MIME

There's no need to open or close an imaginary door in an audition, or drink, or create anything except the innermost struggle of the character in the conflict.

Just be.

11) IT MUST BE MEMORIZED

Never bring in a script when you're supposed to do a monologue for someone. How can the auditioner become involved in the emotion of the monologue if you're not fully connected with it?

Own it. Never walk into an office and take someone's time with a monologue that is not fully prepared. It sends a clear message that you will never be ready for any audition or job you may be sent on.

12) REMAIN IN CHARACTER IN THE LAST MOMENT OF THE MONOLOGUE FOR A FEW BEATS. DON'T JOLT YOUR AUDIENCE OUT OF THE PIECE

A big pet peeve of mine is being jolted back to reality too quickly. After your last line in a monologue, remain in character (perfectly still) for three beats, then finish with a polite "Thank you" *as you, not as the character.*

That gives the auditioner a chance to ease out of the moment, and you a chance to ease out of the audition with politeness and humility.

13) SAY "THANK YOU", NOT "SCENE", OR "THAT'S IT"

After you complete your audition piece, and hold for three seconds (and this may just be a personal preference), "thank you" leaves a better impression on your auditioning audience than blurting out, "scene."

Don't forget that your auditioner is asking in the back of his/her mind, "Can I work with this person? Will we enjoy spending hours in rehearsal together?" If you leave them with a polite, positive salutation, it could become that little edge you may need to land you the role.

No one wants to work with an actor in need of a humility adjustment.

Visualize that the last impression you leave your auditioner with is politeness, respect and humility. Do you think that person will want to work with you? Of course!

First and last impressions leave lasting impressions. How do you wish to be treated for your time? Finishing a monologue with the obvious, "scene," or "that's it" makes me want to respond with "duh!"

14) DON'T RUSH YOUR PERFORMANCE

Actors work so hard to get into a casting director's office, or in front of a producer or director. Why rush the performance?

If you rush what you do, your auditioner will perceive that as a sign of insecurity.

15) WHEN RECEIVING NOTES FROM AN AUDITIONER, JUST LISTEN

It's a habit that many actors have, while receiving notes during an audition, to repeat over and over again, "Uh huh…OK…Uh huh…OK…" Just listen to the note and offer one "thank you" after the auditioner is finished speaking. All that wasted time you spend answering nervously, trying to convince the auditioner that you understand, keeps you from actually absorbing the information.

16) DO YOUR HOMEWORK ON THE PERSON YOU'RE AUDITIONING FOR

Know *the person* you're auditioning for. Research what they've done and future projects. See what you have in common with that person and, if the opportunity arises, make mention of it.

17) POSITION YOURSELF IN A STRONG STANCE AND LEAN FORWARD SLIGHTLY

This gives the actor a physical and psychological edge during a reading or monologue. The auditioner doesn't outwardly absorb what the actor is doing, but subconsciously, it sends a message of confidence.

Conversely, if you sway, lean to either side, or lean back during an audition, it sends a message of insecurity.

Don't believe me? Tape yourself one time and watch. Also, learn by watching the bad or good posture of other performers.

18) DON'T ASK FOR FEEDBACK

After the "thank you," leave. There's no time or need for comments after an audition.

Waiting around for (or asking for) comments displays insecurity. It says, "I'm not a professional yet, so can you throw me a few pointers?" Save that for workshops.

19) DON'T COMMENT WITH AN INSECURE LOOK OR WORDS

We don't know that your monologue went better for you in the shower this morning.

Commenting is also a sign of insecurity. It conveys the message that you're not ready to be hired.

You may think you did the worst audition ever, but you don't know what *the auditioner* is thinking. Politely thank the auditioner and leave, knowing that tomorrow is another day.

20) NO EXCESSIVE CURSING OR MATERIAL THAT IS OFFENSIVE

Unless the character you are auditioning for uses that language, drop the excessive profanity. I guarantee it will offend someone. Offensive, racist material is also discouraged. Why put yourself at a disadvantage? If you're trying to be remembered, it will work, I guarantee it. They'll remember they don't ever want to audition you again.

21) SHOUTING AND SCREAMING ARE NOT MEASURES OF INTENSITY

Actors get all emotionally charged when presenting a monologue and sometimes think that *screaming + shouting=intensity. Shouting=making excessive noise.* What the auditioner is really thinking is, "I hope he doesn't hit or throw something at me," or "I hope the neighbors don't call the police."

Next time you're totally engrossed in a character in a movie or play, ask yourself if it's because the character is ranting, or because of the inward struggle of the character?

22) LEAVE THEM WANTING MORE. 2-3 MINUTES MAX, BUT TAKE YOUR TIME

No matter how well written or well performed the piece may be, three minutes is too long. I used to allow actors to bring in a three-minute monologue (or slightly longer). I have grown to realize that a two to three minute monologue presentation is more than adequate to showcase your ability. If your monologue is longer than that, edit it or work on another piece.

Quality, not quantity.

23) ONLY CHOOSE MONOLOGUES WITHIN YOUR AGE RANGE

That seems obvious, but for some reason, people still bring in pieces that are too old or young for their age range. Work smart on this. If you're twenty-one, no one is going to cast you as a forty year old.

24) SIMPLE IS BEST—FROM THE INSIDE-OUT

Again, stay with the simple truth and honesty of the character. Stay still and deliver your piece *from the inside-out.*

The most interesting feature about you, the feature that every director wants to connect with, and every audience member can relate through, is your eyes.

They are the windows to your soul and emotion pours through them. They are your best tools, so focus and work through the honesty of your emotions (from the inside-out).

Remember, if you are auditioning for a film or television spot, the camera is the director's tool. I guarantee the director will be in the audition room. The director is thinking about how to manipulate the camera for a scene. If you are bouncing off the walls, the director can only think in terms of a master or wide shot to keep up with you. That limits his/her artistic interpretation.

Work through a focused intensity and your stillness will further enhance the director's creativity. The more versatility you allow the director with camera manipulation and angles, the more opportunity you create to be hired.

This business requires a collaborative effort. That can start with your monologue.

25) WHY IS IT TO THE ACTOR'S BENEFIT TO HAVE WRITTEN AN ORIGINAL WORK?

Whether written by you, taken from a work not yet published, or written by someone you know and respect, *no one has seen it before.* It's not *over-used* in the market place.

If I'm watching you, but thinking how much better Johnny Depp was in the role, that's not putting your best foot forward. My opinion of your work as an actor is not influenced totally by what you did, but also by who performed the piece before you.

3

The Six Step Process

STEP ONE: It Must have a beginning, middle and end

Every great story has a beginning, middle and an end. This doesn't mean that you can't leave the audience with a question. This means they should never be left unfulfilled. It's a fine line in creativity.

You may leave your audience wanting more, just don't leave them unfulfilled.

That's like having an intense conversation with the most important person in your life and, for no reason, stopping mid-sentence and walking away. Not only will that person feel unsatisfied, but also a little insulted.

Many times an actor will search and search for that one speech that speaks to the very depth of heart and soul. It's usually a personal need to play a certain character (i.e., the street tough, the victim, the professional, the mobster, etc.). This can be a danger zone if what's chosen is just simply a moment in time, a blurb without a pay off.

In other words, the monologue must stand alone as its own entity.

Whether the auditioning audience has already seen the movie/play or not, you are presenting (in those few minutes) a life and death situation for them to *experience, not just observe.*

Seems obvious, right? It can be subtle, also. If you are trimming dialogue from a piece to cut time down, be sure that you are not losing important story content. You may want to give the product to a coach and ask if the story still translates well.

Have you ever walked out of a film, unfulfilled? Most of the time, if you go back to the credits, you'll find more than one screenwriter listed. There were too many cooks stirring that sauce. That may happen as you modify a piece, so stay aware of this very important concern.

If you end your monologue, leaving auditioners unfulfilled, you haven't completed your task. If you end your monologue with their hearts filled with emotion (the experience complete), but leaving them wanting to see more of your talent, you've done what 98-99% of actors won't take the time to do.

Here it is, folks:

People will forget in an instant what you say, but will remember forever *how you make them feel.*

Without a beginning, middle and end to your monologue, you're playing Russian roulette with your talent. Don't cheat your audience out of an opportunity to feel and experience by leaving them unfulfilled.

STEP TWO: It must be happening in the moment

That means: no "Once upon a times" or "I remember whens."

We want to become part of the conflict in the monologue and experience it with you.

As soon as you go back in time, you become more of a storyteller. At that moment we become less involved in the unfolding action as a participant and more involved as an audience member.

Of course we are audience members to begin with, but we always want feel immersed within the unfolding conflict. You want your auditioner to feel and experience *with* you and not to just listen and watch.

This is part of leaving them wanting more. In the reading of a good book, have you ever needed to put it down for a while and couldn't wait to get back to it? Is it because you had some connection with a specific character? Next time this happens, stop and ask yourself why. Usually it's because the writer is taking you on an *active journey*, unfolding moment by moment. You, as the reader have now become a *participant*.

Next time you're watching a movie that has you on the edge of your seat, consider if, at that moment in time, the character is in the middle of a story about the past, or within the throes of a current dilemma.

Going back to *explain* the past, or how a character made it to the current situation is considered *exposition* in a script. A writer has this luxury when preparing to tell a larger story. You want to avoid this as much as possible for a 2-3 minute monologue.

Avoid back-story by beginning *at the height* of the conflict.

THE TICKING CLOCK

The fact that the monologue can only occur at this moment (the moment of truth) is what creates a ticking clock, a story device found in the best scripts.

What do I mean by that? A ticking clock is a *built-in time device* to create suspense and intrigue.

An *ultimatum* may be planted in the dialogue to enhance that ticking clock.

The director will also visually present the ticking clock through the action of the story. For an example of that, let's consider a scene in *Titanic*, the film by James Cameron. Mr. Cameron is a big fan and master of the ticking clock technique. He uses it in everything he writes. There's a great reason for that:

The ticking clock is what keeps the audience on the edge of their seats more effectively than anything else.

Remember the scene in *Titanic* when Jack (Leonardo DiCaprio) is handcuffed to a pipe? The water is clearly seen rising out the little window next to him, while Rose (Kate Winslet) is searching for help. She finds the axe, swims back to him and has to chop at the handcuffs to free her lover.

What is the device that creates the ticking clock? The rising water. That means that the scene can only take place at this moment. Thus, we are at the edge of our seats, hoping that she can save him in time so the two lovers have a better opportunity to survive together.

The sinking ship is the overall *ticking clock* in the story. However, Mr. Cameron uses that device to create smaller ticking clocks. Because most of the story occurs within a confined area (the ship), he has created smaller ticking clocks with the use of sub-plots (i.e., whether or not the two lovers will escape together, whether or not Rose's fiancé will shoot one or both of them, whether Rose will stay on the life boat as it is descending to the water) to insure that we stay right where he wants us, on the edge of our seats. He strategically weaves them through the overall spine of the story.

Look also to *The Abyss,* another of Mr. Cameron's films, for a wonderful ticking clock in a confined area. See if you can locate a very similar situation where the water is rising while the two lovers struggle to survive.

I use both of those examples to support the importance of creating a situation (the ticking clock), which *captivates* an audience. The most successful monologues embrace the ticking clock device to captivate an audience.

STEP THREE: Talk to just one person

Have you ever experienced two people having a conversation in front of you about someone you don't know, have never met, and will probably never meet? How does that make you feel? A little abandoned? That's the way your auditioner feels as soon as you begin talking about a character they don't know, who is not in the room and will never enter the room.

Include the auditioner in the piece. Leave third parties out of your work. Your auditioner needs to feel like the person you are talking to (even though you may not be performing the monologue directly to them).

As soon as your character says, "I was talking with Joe the other day and he said…" We don't know Joe and don't care to know Joe during these two minutes where a decision is being made about your career. Joe is not the person the monologue is directed towards. There is no time to explain or introduce Joe in this moment.

The monologue, to be truly effective, only has the luxury of containing a protagonist and antagonist. Adding another person (a catalyst) only confuses the person watching the monologue.

Keep the conflict between you and the person you're talking to in the monologue, and keep it in the moment.

STEP FOUR: Must be life or death

- **Life or death of a relationship**
- **The threat of serious physical harm (death)**
- **Life or death of an emotion**

That's it.

The most misunderstood of the three is *life or death of an emotion.* We know what life or death of a relationship is, or if someone has a gun or knife on you, it's easy to figure that your physical life is in danger.

But, what does *life or death of an emotion* mean? While the first two deal with the threat of direct action against another, the third is more inward.

In other words, you're threatening to retreat inside yourself as a means of affecting your relationship with another person.

Let's say we have a troubled character, someone who has been abused in some way. This person has decided to reach out for help or to confront the abuser one last time. If this character doesn't receive satisfaction in some way, then he/she has decided to pull the love and respect for that person away forever. That is life or death of an emotion.

Example:

> Mom, this is the last time I'm going to share how I feel about how badly you treat me when you're drunk. If you ever pour another drink again, I'll never share how I feel again.

You have to make sure the stakes are the highest they can possibly be in this moment.

If two people are having a conversation about the weather, how interesting is that? However, if one person is leaving a relationship, but looking for one last reason to stay and try again (due to their mutual love), that is interesting.

But, what about comedy? Can that also be life or death?

Absolutely. The *device* that creates comedy in life or death situations is *irony*.

Every great story has it.

Here's an example: Picture a financially desperate man about to rob his first bank. He's terrified. He pulls a pistol on the teller. The teller, distraught with her own life, smiles, pulls a pistol from her purse and points it at herself. He has a pistol pointed at her and now she has one pointed at herself.

She says, "Isn't that something, I brought this today and figured I was going to shoot myself right after finishing your transaction." She removes her life savings from her purse and hands it to him—a wad of money she has saved up over the years. She tells him he can't have the bank money though.

He tucks his pistol away in his jacket and proceeds to try and convince the teller to take her money back and put her pistol away. He explains that, "things can't be *that bad* in her life." At the end of the piece, he asks her to dinner because she is the first selfless person he has met in a long time. His desperation turned into attraction with the use of *irony*.

Can this be a good monologue? You bet. The drama is created through the danger (threat of physical harm). The ticking clock is created through the appearance of the pistols. The irony of the teller turning the tables on the robber creates the comedy. That's what makes us laugh, whether in belly-laugh farce, situation comedy, or in a more subtle comic moment.

STEP FIVE: Must be founded in love

This is possibly the most important part of the process, and many times the part that becomes overlooked the most in an actor's preparation.

In Michael Shurtleff's book, *Audition*, he asks, "Where is the love?" It's very much the same issue here.

All of your work must be founded in love. Make that choice and you make the choice to connect with your audience.

If the main conflict in any piece surrounds a matter of the heart, that struggle is one that your audience will become the most emotionally attached to. The reason for that is we are emotional beings first.

We go to the theatre, become lost in a film, or get caught up in a good book because we emotionally connect with the characters.

When James Cameron's movie, *Titanic*, was released, someone encouraged me to see it immediately. I said, "I already know the ending. The ship goes down." He said, "No that's the back-story for the love story." My friend was absolutely right. What made it exciting, intriguing and kept me at the edge of my seat, was the constant threat of the two lovers not being together at the end of the film.

What's the strongest emotion? Love. Don't think for a second it might be fear, hate, anger, etc. They are all by-products of love. If you cannot love, you will not experience any of those other emotions.

Love is the universal connector between all human beings, so it only stands to reason that it should be the underlying emotion in a monologue.

OK, what if you're talking to a murderer who has you at gunpoint in the monologue? Do you love that person? My question is how strong is your love for yourself, or someone else? What is your purpose for living and what is your innermost fear, if not to live for yourself or another relationship?

It comes down to *specific intent*, and I speak of that often.

Specific intent creates how you react, based on the inner-monologue of your piece. The inner-monologue is the voice in your head, struggling with that heart-felt life or death decision.

I was involved in the auditioning process in a Los Angeles film studio in the late 1980s. We were auditioning women for the lead in a short film. The director wanted to audition them with only these two words, "You bastard." That was it. It was the last line of a highly emotional confrontation; after the femme fatale discovered her fiancé was giving her an unfair ultimatum, based solely on his fears.

The director didn't want the scene; he just wanted her last line. What was worse for the actresses that were auditioning was that he wouldn't provide any of the dialogue that occurred before that line to their agents. So, we sat that day through a multitude of angry, frustrated, bitter and resentful versions of those two words. There were arms flailing, shouting, stamping of feet, sweating, angry heavy breathing, etc., etc., etc.

Finally (I believe it was the last scheduled audition of the day), an actress entered and stood perfectly still. The room went silent as she remained for what seemed to be minutes, just allowing emotion to begin to over-take her (from the inside out).

As she held back the tears, she barely said, in a very loving way, "You bastard." She then took another minute to compose herself.

After we wiped our eyes, guess who got the role? We knew the line, yet she connected with us at the place where we can all relate. She pulled us into her emotional struggle as the character.

Remember that I said that she *held the tears back.*

If she had poured out the tears, we would have watched and probably all agreed that it was a good performance. She held her tears back, which allowed *us* to cry. Watching someone at the height of adversity, trying to handle an emotional situation (with strength and courage), affects our emotions far greater than someone who gives us everything.

Next time you watch a love story, make note of what makes you cry. Your tears usually flow when a character is struggling to accept (many times through humor, but always through holding back tears) a heart-wrenching situation with courage and integrity.

So, always choose *love* for the foundation in the struggle of any character you develop. We'll show examples of this in the following pages.

STEP SIX: Must be three minutes or less

We spoke about this before and I'll stress it once again. **Leave them wanting more.** Allow them to ask you to stay. You do that by giving them *a taste* of your abilities.

Can you see why I love the monologue so much? Those of you who still think monologues are useless, consider this:

With the monologue, *you* control the audition. You control:

    1) their emotions

    2) how much you offer in the given time to tease their decision-making

    3) the opportunity to offer more than most actors who walk through the door. You've been able to prepare longer, in more depth and make the most of the opportunity at hand

Have you heard the expression, *"Timing is everything?" You* control it in the audition.

In any audition, you *can't* control whether you're too fat for the role, too skinny, too tall, too short, too blonde, brunette, bald, etc., etc., etc. You *can* control your work and the timing of it. Isn't that why you're there in the first place?

Make it count.

4

Original Monologues

Let's present some monologues. We'll rate each piece according to the Six Step Process. Not every piece will meet all six steps, every time.

Before we start, let's understand that just because a monologue doesn't meet every step, it doesn't mean the piece won't work for you. Just understand that with *each step it lacks*, the *strength* of the monologue is weakened just a little more.

The most impacting monologue is one that contains each of the Six Steps defined, and can instill feelings of heartfelt joy *and* sadness in the same experience.

Warning: Whether someone laughs or cries is not the point. Each person expresses emotions differently; so don't judge the effectiveness of your performance on whether your auditioner reacts with tears or great laughter.

Many of the monologues you will read in this chapter are *genderless.*

Comedy-Baby S__t is filled with irony and supports most of the Six Steps, plus it evokes joy and sadness.

BABY S__T

By Peter DeAnello

Get married? Oh...Uh...Thank you...I mean, I'm flattered...Not flattered, but...Sit down, please. I knew this was going to come up sooner or later. I've got something to tell you. (Searching) You know how people sometimes expect the worst, but the worst is sometimes worse than the worst they expected? Now you're really worried. You know how you and I talk about things we want, you'll say, "a house in the mountains", and I'll say, "To win the lotto for a mill..." Do you know what I really want more than anything else in the world? I want just one dirty diaper. One that belongs to *me*! Not *my* diaper, a baby's...which gets me back to what I'm trying to talk about. *Baby shit*! I want to be drooled on, spit up on, teethed on...I want to kiss a bruised knee and make it all better. I welcome bloodshot eyes! I want to wake up at 2:00 AM to <u>my</u> screaming baby, just to know that when she falls back asleep, it's because she's in the security of her father's (mother's) arms. But what *I really* want is to look in that baby's eyes and see the reflection of you *and me*!

We'll never be able to look in our baby's eyes. The best way to say this is that nature didn't give me the ability inside to make one...(a long uncomfortable beat, no response) Uh...You can talk now...(still no response). Look, the way I see it is you don't even have to say much! Just pick, A, B, or C...Uh...A, you could ask me to leave right now...B, We can go ahead with getting, you know, married...And C, you can sue me for wasting the last six years of your life! (silence) I'll give you a minute to think about it...I'll, uh...wait outside...

(Starts to leave, suddenly turns back)

Huh? "B"? Uh...I forgot what "B" was.

Let's review the Six Steps and understand what makes this work:

1) Does it have a beginning, middle and end? Absolutely, but does it also leave the audience thinking? Yes, not unfulfilled, but still thinking.

2) Is it talking to just one person? Yes, but here is where it falls a little short. The baby becomes the third party. You may argue, "But, that's what the monologue is about." You're right, but it diminishes conflict between the two speaking parties by adding another whom we don't know. Also, the real question here between them is, "Are you going to marry me, or not?"

3) Is it happening in the moment? It has to, because marriage has just been proposed.

4) It is life or death of a relationship.

5) Is it founded in love? Absolutely.

6) Is it three minutes or under? Yes, at the proper pacing. What is the proper pacing? Think about this person, nervous, at this place and time-you'll understand.

Think about the irony in this comic situation. Does anyone really want to be spit up on? Teethed on? Drooled on?

Can you find any other ironies?

Black Comedy—Daddy teases the seriousness of the mobster genre. It falls short of the Six Steps with references to third parties and the past (once upon a time).

DADDY

By Peter DeAnello

I know there's a taxi outside! Because, I'm leaving—for good! That's right, gone, kaput, nada. What better time than on my 26th birthday? It's time, don't you think? Curse all you want, then go into the (Italian accent, hands waving) "You gotta no respect!" speech.

Because, I'd like to keep a boyfriend, Daddy, that's why. Nobody will *ever* be good enough for you. That's why I'm leaving. That, and because of all the mysterious disappearances of every guy I've ever had a *first* date with. No, it's not about them, it's about you and me! I want just <u>one</u> second date in my life. I know you love me…too much. I know you want to protect me…too much. Because of you, my life is a Disney Movie, rated "G"-bring the kids! Hell, bring the neighbor's kids!

Daddy, stop crying. I'm not falling for the "Since your mother died" speech either. You've got a choice. You can admit to and apologize for fifteen disappearances, and promise it will never happen again, or I walk out now…

Good. That's a start…Sixteen? Who was…? Never mind. And, you promise to start trusting me? Let me hear you say it…Good. I love you too, Daddy. (She starts to leave) Huh? Oh, I'm just going out to tell my new boyfriend I'm staying…He drives a taxi and…(she looks out the window) Daddy? Where is he? The taxi's there, but he's not! That better not be number Sixteen! Don't you look away!

Let's review this one:

1) It has a beginning, middle and end.

2) It is happening in the moment, except for the discussion of past boyfriends.

3) Is it talking to just one person? Yes, but there are third parties discussed, i.e., boyfriends and mother. That takes our attention off thinking about just their relationship with each other.

4) It is life or death of a relationship.

5) It is founded in love.

6) It is three minutes or under.

Drama—Seasons was a monologue that developed into a play. Though it was written for a woman, it is genderless.

SEASONS

By Peter DeAnello

Michael...Elizabeth, since I don't know which one you're going to be, I have some good news for you and some bad news...The good news is...I'm your mother. The bad, well, you're never going to know me, except through this video. See, I have to go and live where you came from. I'm not a speaker, and I've never been a mom, so bear with me...How do you pack a million years of love, greater than life itself into a few moments? There are a few things I want to say...First, (joking), listen to your father. Sorry, I had to say that just once...Second, baby, you're going to make a lot of mistakes in life. Learn from them. Your mother made a lot of mistakes...Cancer wasn't one of them. It just happened. But, I'm not here to preach to you, just to make you a promise...No matter who you are or what you become, I'll be here with you every step of the way. You may not see me, but I'm here...with you now, as you watch this. And I want you to make me a promise. Talk to me? I'm listening. You don't even have to say it loud, just whisper it in your heart, because that's where mommy is living now. (She composes herself)

Make every day important. Live it. Breathe it. Embrace it. Because you'll never know what tomorrow will bring. I can go now, but if I leave knowing I'll never be forgotten, I'll have accomplished what every parent hopes to accomplish in a lifetime. And, just so you never throw it up to me and say, "She never said she loved me"...I love you...With all my heart...And don't be frightened if you feel a soft kiss brush your cheek as you fall asleep at night...It's just mommy, saying goodnight.

1) It has a beginning, middle and end.

2) It is happening in the moment as well as in the future—*Irony.*

3) She is talking to just one person, though mentioning the father.

4) It surrounds life or death of a relationship.

5) It is totally founded in love.

6) It is three minutes or under.

Farce—Dr. Rightmind is a fun piece, filled with irony.

DR. RIGHTMIND

By Peter DeAnello

Dr. Rightmind, thank you for seeing me again on such short notice, especially after just being released from intensive care. I've been having a tremendous bout with conscience after, well, almost biting your face off last time. I heard that plastic surgeon did wonders. Can you really see me through all those bandages? (motioning with her fingers) One means yes, two means no...Good.

I know in our last session, before our "incident," I told you I loved you and it frightened you because of the mysterious disappearances of my former...well, that's all water under the bridge anyway. Who knows, maybe they'll float up, I mean, "show" up again...some day...and finally dispel all those doubting Thomases.

The truth is, Doctor, *you* told me I could say anything to you, that whatever would be discussed or happened between us would remain between us. Well, you big hunk of...(squinting to see his face) gauze and tape...Wouldn't that sound like a bit more than a patient/doctor relationship to you? Admit that you started it! Go ahead now, tell the truth and spite the devil. One means yes, two means no...Good.

Look, you bundle of blood stained cotton and gauze, I know I came to you for anger management, but I believe that through falling in love with you, I've finally understood the real me! You've opened up the very essence of my being! It's so clear to me now. Can you guess what it is? It's the reason why, after you wouldn't let me kiss you, I bit off almost every protruding facial appendage! I HAVE AN ORAL FIXATION! Isn't that great? And because of you, I realize it! See? Only true love can produce that kind of revelation! Can you blame me? You're just so cute and pudgy, I could just swallow you up...

(She gets up to approach him and backs off again)

OK, you big baby, it was a joke. (she cringes, then looks down) See, of course you didn't see that big old file cabinet. Are you OK, sweetie? One means yes, two...that's right.

(She sits again) You better not have ruined that new nose the doctors worked so hard on! Cause, when you get better I have a big surprise for you! I'm going to prove to you that this same mouth that caused you three hundred and fifty one stitches...Huh? Excuse me, three hundred fifty six stitches on the top end of your body can create a different kind of havoc on other parts...Now you tell me if that's not something to look forward to—you big lollipop!

1) It has a beginning middle and end.

2) It is happening in the moment.

3) It is speaking to just one person.

4) It is life or death of a relationship as well as the threat of physical death.

5) It is founded in love.

6) Here's where it may hurt. It isn't three minutes or under.

Drama—The Visit supports all Six Steps.

THE VISIT

By Peter DeAnello

(He/she approaches quietly and sits, gazing at the person in bed, asleep)

You're just as beautiful asleep. Keep dreaming, but just listen. If tomorrow you wake up and consider this just a dream, that's OK, as long as you remember this visit.

I know you didn't invite me. I hope you don't mind.

I needed to confess this (leans in, whispering) I...Love you. I always have. I have another confession...I always sang that song that you love *to you*. I can only hope that whenever you hear it from now on, that you always think of me, and only me.

Keep it ours, even if it's only in friendship. (He/she looks to the side and smiles sadly) I have to go. See, there's a light that just keeps getting brighter. It seems to be calling me somehow. Don't ask me how I know that, it just has a will of it's own (starts to get up, stops and sits again).

Speaking of that, you *can* have what you want. You can *will* it, if you want it bad enough. I know that *now*, because as I looked down at my body after the accident just now, and that light started beckoning me to follow. I refused to follow it, that is, until I could see you one more time. I willed it.

If you will something with all your heart, all your mind and soul, you can have it. (joking sadly) I'm living proof. Just arrived at that too late.

If it's OK with you, I'm going to concentrate real hard, till the time the light beckons you too. Wherever it takes me, I'll save a place for you there, in my arms. Somehow, some way, could you find a way to let me know if that's OK, cause if it is, I know I can wait. I'll just hold my arms out for a lifetime, if it takes that long.

(He/she gets up and nods towards the light, singing through streaming tears) "You'd be like Heaven to touch, I want to hold you so much. At long last love has arrived and I thank God I'm alive. (he/she turns and starts towards the light until off stage, singing) You're just too good to be true, can't take my eyes off of you…"

1) It has a beginning, middle and end.

2) It is happening in the moment.

3) It is speaking to just one person.

4) It is life or death of a relationship.

5) It is founded in love.

6) It is three minutes.

This story, though more dramatic than the others, is also filled with irony. Think about it.

Drama—*Forget Me* is a good example that supports all Six Steps. It is also genderless, but better fitted to a woman.

FORGET ME

By Peter DeAnello

I am not sneaking out. OK, I am…I could tell you, but I'd have to kill you. No, this time I'm not laughing. I love you. That's why I'm leaving. I can only tell you that I'm needed for another assignment. You have to forget me. Please don't ask for more than that. Forget what you're feeling now. Forget how you love me like no person has ever loved me in my life. I *have* to forget you, Jimmy, and I will, for your sake. Please don't ever try to contact me again because you will never find me. I'll have a new name, a new address and a new husband.

I don't mean to stare. It always happens the same way. We'll forget little pieces at a time of each other. But you…I have to hold on to the picture, the memory of you for as long as I can…Your little boy blue eyes that melt me, your shy grin…Your kind heart.

I don't expect you to understand. I'm betraying you through necessity. I lied to you through fear, but never of you. I'm sorry for all that I put you through. You deserve better than me, Jimmy, but not because I don't love you with all my heart. Please take my face in your hands and kiss me one more time?

(She closes her tear-filled eyes and waits—nothing) I don't blame you. Go on, Jimmy. I *will* go on, I promise. And I'll love again—I'll have to, because it's my job, but I'll never love again like this.

   1) It has a beginning, middle and end.

   2) It is happening in the moment.

   3) It is talking to just one person.

4) It is life or death of a relationship.

5) It is founded in love.

6) It is three minutes or under.

Comedy—It is steeped in irony and love, but contains third party references.

THE RUSH

By Peter DeAnello

Oh, Joey, this is the happiest day of my…(noticing his finger) Excuse me, where's your ring? The one I just slipped on your finger in front of God, our families & friends, and about two hundred members of gamblers anonymous!

You did what? Say that again? Who? You get that ring back! He won't break your legs. He's our minister. (She starts to figure it out) Joey? Where did you *find* the good reverend? Our lady of WHAT? No, let me…*Our Lady of I'll break your legs if you don't pay me,* right?

Reverend "Marker"…I'm so stupid…Joey, you promised! Here, take *my* ring too! (She checks her finger, there's no ring). Well, that's convenient. Any one of the hundreds of people who just hugged and shook my hand could have it. It's probably being melted down in the vestibule right now. Maybe I should check to make sure my garter is still on?

When does it end, Joey? When you gamble away my heart, my soul, my…(a realization) Uh oh. This is not good. No, it's not the rings, or the minister. I always thought you'd be the first, Joey. Yes, you married a virgin. I kept *my* promise, but you won't be the first to *have me*. At the rehearsal dinner last night, we were all drinking and your best man bet me that you couldn't make it to the cutting of the cake without making a bet. I took the bet, Joey. I put up my virginity as collateral.

I wanted to see what the big deal was about making a bet. I never, for a moment, thought I would lose it to *him*! I believed in you. (She starts to leave, then pauses and smiles) But, you know, you're right, there is kind of a *rush* to it. I'll meet you for the toast.

1) It has a beginning, middle and end.

2) It is happening in the moment, however, there is a reference to yesterday.

3) It's talking to one person, but mentioning the reverend and the best man. Both are third party references.

4) Is it really life or death? There is a sacrifice, but not life or death, so although it is fun and light, the audience is not on the edge of their seats.

5) It is founded in love.

6) It is three minutes or less.

Drama—Nino is deeply founded in love, but falls short because it's not life or death in the moment. It refers to the past and it contains third party references.

NINO

By Peter DeAnello

It's funny, doctor, before the baby was born, my husband and I argued about everything, from the color of the paint in the room to where the crib should go. We wanted to make sure everything was perfect for our perfect baby. I couldn't sleep last night. I kept thinking back to the old neighborhood. There was a little boy named Nino. He lived a few houses down from us. Nino had Down's Syndrome.

He had a crush on me for most of our childhood. I played with him when we were toddlers, then I realized he was *different*. I kept thinking last night about this one day. I was twelve, walking home from school with some friends. Nino was waiting for me, standing by my mailbox. His hair was combed. He never combed his hair. He had a bouquet of freshly picked daisies in his hand from his mother's garden. He was probably waiting all day to give them to me.

As he held them out to me, his hand was shaking. I was in front of my girl-friends…peer pressure, I guess. I slapped them out of his hand and they fell to the ground. I didn't want to do that. They laughed at him as he ran home. I couldn't laugh. I watched him run up to his mother and she hugged him on the porch. She just looked at me, hurt. He wasn't crying. I never saw him cry. But, as she held him close, tears streamed from her eyes down the back of his shirt.

Nino never approached me after that. Paul and I visited the old neighborhood about a year ago. I saw Nino walking home with groceries and waved. He just put his head down and kept walking.

This morning I spoke to Nino's mother on the phone. As soon as we leave the hospital today, we're driving to the old neighborhood. I'm finally going to thank Nino for those daisies and give him a bouquet of my own. Then, I'm going to ask his mother to prepare us for what's ahead for Carolyn Marie…She smiled at me for the first time today.

1) This has a beginning, middle and end.

2) It is not happening in the moment. Although it's a good story that is heartfelt, the audience won't be on the edge of their seats.

3) Though she is talking to just one person, there are third parties mentioned. The audience doesn't know the mother, husband, or Nino. So, they're left waiting for explanations and descriptions.

4) Here is an example of life or death of an emotion. Nino never approached her again. There could be a good argument for life or death of a relationship here also.

5) Here is what makes the piece so appealing. It is founded in love, as it contains hurt, frustration and guilt, due to love.

6) It is three minutes or under.

Comedy—Through irony. *The Shuffle* is a good example of how to turn around a situation and present comedy through irony. It falls short because there are third party references and it mentions past experiences.

THE SHUFFLE

By Peter DeAnello

Well, to tell you the truth, Mr. Morris, it got so ridiculous after a while…It all started when I moved to New York a few years back, to pursue my dream…to drive a cab. Hey, I always wanted to drive a cab. Great job. How else could you see all of Manhattan in one day, park anywhere you like, and not be confined behind a desk? People were fighting for that job.

Anyway, that's when they all started just appearing from everywhere. Producers, directors, agents…"Wanna be in a movie?" "Wanna be on a soap?" "Hey, kid, lotta money in doing commercials." I looked at them all like they were nuts. "And give up all this?" I mean, let's be serious, I like the smell of soot on a hot sticky day, dodging double parked cars, traffic and shit. Get outta here!

But, they kept getting in my cab on every corner, contracts in hand. I swear it was a conspiracy. It got so bad that I stopped picking anyone up anymore. So, what do you think I did? What would you do? I moved out of there I went to LA, to be a waiter.

Hey, my mother always wanted me to be a waiter. Great job, benefits, plus you can learn a variety of languages. So, there I was, working on my feet twelve hours a day, having a ball, you know? Who do you think comes in one night? Sly Stallone. The first words out of his mouth were, "Yo, you wanna fight me in "Rocky Eight?" I said, "Yo, Sly, you've been hit too many times…And give up all this?"

But, did it stop there? Word got out…Producers, directors, casting directors, agents…It got so the place was always packed with them. Now, let's be serious here, what would you do if you were trying to manage a restaurant where no one could get a seat because of you? Of course they fired me. They had to.

But, it didn't stop there. People in LA are vicious. They found out where I lived! I had to put a sign on my door that read, "Please slide your requests for my picture and resume under the door."

The bottom line here is, now I'm broke. Nobody wants to hire me because of the crowds. Hey, if you can't beat em, join em, you know? So, Mr. Morris, if you really want to represent me…I admit it, you guys win…Why not? (After a long beat, pleading.) Please?

1) It has a beginning, middle and end.

2) It is not always totally in the moment, because the piece has history.

3) It is talking to one person, but refers to third parties.

4) It is life or death in the moment.

5) It is not founded in love, except for self.

6) It is three minutes or less.

Auditioners may think it's clever, but they're watching a story unfold and can't become personally invested in a life or death situation.

Farce-Here's a fun niche, seasonal monologue.

THE TWELFTH DAY OF CHRISTMAS

By Peter DeAnello

Do you know what this is, Harry? Besides the twelfth day of Christmas. It's the day I kill you! Why? Because, you've made me a mental case! You're a lunatic, and I love you, but you're overly generous! It stops here! Today, I put you out of my misery. Why?

Let's start with the partridge in the pear tree…Odd, but cute! Then two turtle doves arrive…I figured you were on a bird kick…Excessive, but sweet, that is until the doves ate Sam! Who's Sam?—the partridge! I had feathers all over the place! On day three, I kept asking myself, what the hell am I going to do with three French hens? Or four calling birds…I still haven't figured out what a calling bird is. At least if you're giving me a gift, let me know what it is, so I can explain it to the landlord at the eviction hearing!

Five golden rings redeemed you for a day, until…Geese, Harry!? Laying eggs all over the place! They stink and have the worst disposition in the world. But what the hell, after that, I had swans swimming in the tub, toilet and sink, maids milking cows in the living room, lords leaping on the maids, and nine horny pipers blowing accompaniment to the Rockettes in my basement. Today, I saw twelve drummers coming down the street and locked my door. That's why I'm here, Harry. I love you, but if I don't kill you, I know I'll have rabbits delivered at my door in four months and black cats in October!

1) It has a beginning, middle and end.

2) It's downfall is that most of what occurs is in the past. That detracts from the action of the piece occurring in the moment.

3) It is talking to just one person, however references are made to others.

4) It is life or death of a relationship and the threat of physical harm.

5) I encourage the actor to make choices in love and not just anger.

6) It is three minutes or under.

This is a good example of a niche monologue. It can be a seasonal monologue. However, since its genre is *Farce*, it would be better used in a specific situation.

Drama—With a touch of thriller. This is a good niche monologue.

THE NEW UNDERSTANDING

By Peter DeAnello

I hope that duct tape isn't wrapped too tight. You can breathe, and that's what's important, Sam. If you can breathe, you can listen. You promised you weren't going to drink again. How did I know you did? See this bruise over my eye? You don't remember doing that, do you? I didn't think so. I know it hurts to talk. I took the scissors and snipped off a little piece of your tongue for lying to me. You'll learn to talk without that itsy bitsy piece…And, if you lie again, another little bit goes. The bandage on your hand is because I found the vodka in the freezer this morning, frozen. Did you think you would really get away with watering it down? So, I cut off your thumb. If you can't grab the bottle, you can't hold it.

If I can't have the whole man, I'll have to settle for whatever is left that's still good.

Right? And, that's where we're at now. We're developing a little *understanding*, because I love you and lying to, or beating on me, are unacceptable. If I didn't love you, Sam, I would have to just slit your throat when you were sleeping. But I do love you and we're going to spend the rest of our lives together, happy.

So, you will remain in this basement, taped up, until you're thinking straight again. Then I will take that shovel and smash it into your eye, so you will know what this feels like. When you heal, you will go to AA at least three times a week for the rest of your life, because the one thing we know is that you'll always be an alcoholic. If you miss even one meeting, I'll divorce you and then you'll never get rid of me…Because, if I have to live without the man I love, the man I love just won't live. This makes me so happy! How many couples that meet and marry in just one week understand each other so well? I love you.

1) It has a beginning, middle and end.

2) It is happening in the moment, though she talks a bit about the night before.

3) It's just between the two people.

4) It carries the physical threat of death and life or death of the relationship.

5) If it is founded in love, it makes this piece more threatening.

6) It is three minutes or under.

Drama—Here's irony in a dramatic situation where the victim turns the tables.

THE VICTIM

By Peter DeAnello

(Struggling to hold her head high and proud) Thank you for seeing me. I thought you might be out celebrating your victory. I have a few reasons for making an appointment to see you, first to congratulate you on winning your case against me. I just wonder if building your career on innocent rape victims is something that an attorney dreams about in law school? Or, was I the reason for taking the case in the first place? Your smirk suggests that this might make us even. But, does having your heart broken by your ex-fiancé justify winning a rape case against her later?

Here's something else to gloat over. I suspect my husband is leaving me over this. I guess you were that convincing. Finally, I wanted to explain why I left you so quickly ten years ago.

I loved you so much more than you know. Whether you believe it or not, I didn't want to interfere with what you loved most. Doing anything else but law would have destroyed you. I knew that. I realized it when I visited to the office late one night and found you with the firm owner's daughter. I came that night to surprise you with the news that I was pregnant. I know you didn't see me, so I just slipped out back. When you returned home I was gone, no note, and you got to play the victim for the last ten years.

So, I had a baby boy, and married a wonderful man. We were happy, until this. (She gets up to leave) You'll want a DNA test for the child support hearing.

1) It has a beginning, middle and end.

2) It suffers from not totally happening in the moment.

3) Though talking to one person, it suffers when she refers to her husband, their son and the attorney's ex-lover.

4) It is life or death of a relationship, but unfortunately not of the relationship between the two people involved.

5) It is founded in love, but only if the actress chooses hurt more than revenge.

6) It is three minutes or under.

I believe the really powerful monologue in this scenario exists between the husband and wife, at the moment when the husband is leaving. Let's write that one:

THE VICTIM—PART 2

By Peter DeAnello

Were you waiting to say goodbye, or did I just come home sooner than you expected? I noticed the car was packed, with the engine idling. Even my husband seems to think I'm guilty by suspicion. I get raped and everyone goes free but me. I run in the park on my lunch hour so of course I deserve what I get. Even my husband feels that way. Fine. (She waits for him to leave. He remains) Sorry I spoiled the surprise. Just go. There's nothing left to explain. (He remains) Don't torture me Jerry, looking for some kind of permission or exoneration. Just leave. I don't have the strength to fight you. All I have left is what I can pull from the depth of my soul to go on with again, knowing that whatever anyone believes, I didn't ask to be raped. I married you for the rest of my life.

I understand if you have doubts, and if I'm worth staying for, I'll work those out with you. I would work for as long as takes because I've promised myself to you. No experience or violation could change that, no matter what. I'm sorry if you don't feel the same way. The door is open, Jerry, but please don't come back. Whatever your decision is, please make it final.

(He still remains) You have to go out there, no matter what. I'll stay right here. If the car is turned off, we begin again. If I hear the door shut and you leave, I wish you love beyond what you have for me, because it wasn't enough. (She steps aside and waits)

    1) This has a beginning, middle and end.

    2) It is happening in the moment, though there is some reference to the past.

    3) It is just between the two people.

    4) It is life or death of a relationship

    5) It is founded in love.

    6) It is three minutes or under.

We've taken a look at the violation from a different point of view. Now, let's write it from the husband's point of view.

Here is also an example of an open-ended monologue that doesn't leave the auditioner unfulfilled.

THE VICTIM—PART THREE

By Peter DeAnello

I left the car idling while I've been waiting for you to come home. I don't know if after I explain my feelings that I'll leave or stay. That sounds insensitive, I know.

What do you want to hear, Sarah? That I haven't sat and wondered if you didn't invite the rape? You've always been a flirt and I've asked you so many times not to jog in that area of the park and wear such skimpy outfits. Does that justify rape? Of course it doesn't.

I know I'm not supposed to say, "I told you so", but I'm bitter and resentful...And hurt. And, I feel selfish saying those things, because it didn't happen to me, but it did.

I love you, Sarah, and I'm understanding and supportive, but I can't hold inside what I feel. After this, will you still continue to just shrug off my warnings with, "Stop being controlling", or "You're over-possessive?" I know we can't go back, and I never wanted our marriage to be about living in confinement.

If I stay, I can't say that those things won't eat at me. I'll turn off the car, for now.

    1) This has a beginning, middle and end, even though it leaves the audience questioning if their relationship will survive.

    2) It is happening in the moment.

    3) It is just between the two people.

    4) It is life or death of a relationship.

    5) It is founded in love.

6) It is three minutes or under.

You can see that writing your own monologue allows you the freedom to change the scene, or reverse it at will. This frees the actor to create the perspective that works best.

By just following the Six Steps, the sky's the limit.

Comedy—Through Irony. Here is an example of how serious comedy is.

JOE

By Peter DeAnello

It's time for you to get your own place, Joe. I won't stand for another night that you don't come home, especially with another female's smell on you. I hear that door at night when you try to sneak home without trying to wake me. That door swings both ways, you know. I'm sorry, but I'm not going to share you. I know you didn't have anything when we met, but you've been taking advantage of me ever since. You don't do anything all day but parasite off me. You haven't even ventured out to see if there's anything you *can* do. I just come home to food all over the place and a messy house. God forbid I didn't put a lock on that refrigerator! Look at your weight, Joe. You don't respect yourself anymore. How could you respect me?

I just want you to know that I will miss you lying next to me in bed. I'll miss your warmth and your kisses. What I won't miss, Joe, are the nights you don't come home. I won't miss the messy house or your disregard for my feelings.

I didn't mind being the breadwinner in this relationship, I just didn't want to be taken advantage of. It's always about your needs. Won't you even fight for me? (No response) Fine, I've packed your things. You can stay in the new guest quarters out back. Decorate it however you want, or not. It can be as messy as you want. And, if you have a guest over, I don't want to know about it. Just make sure she's gone by morning. Just make sure she comes with her own pooper-scooper. Now, you can carry your own bowl out there.

1) This has a beginning, middle and end.

2) It is happening in the moment.

3) Talking to one "person."

4) It is life or death of a relationship.

5) It is founded in love.

6) It is three minutes or under

Drama—Weighing the scales of justice.

THE DILEMA

By Peter DeAnello

Who do you think you are, Elliott Ness? Do you think a badge makes you right all of a sudden? We have a little dilemma, don't we? If you're serious, you better fire that thing, cause my best friend in the world isn't turning in his chips on us unless it's all the way. So, if you're not one hundred percent serious and committed to this, put that gun away or I'll forget how much I love you.

We've gotta understand what's right, here. What's right is with us, Louie. It's that I'd kill *for* you. I wouldn't *kill you*. Know what a difference those three letters, *for* means? They make the difference between the one thing in life that most people screw up...*Loyalty* beyond rules and regulations, beyond what someone else thinks is right and wrong. It's the difference between *guessing* about someone, or *knowing* that you never let them walk behind you, or that you never have to frisk them, or have their house searched, or their phone bugged to make sure they won't turn on you. I don't want to worry about your next move or who you're whispering to in dark alleys, or in corners of noisy restaurants!

You're family! The only thing you did right just now is that you put the gun to my chest and not my back. Is this the best you can do for us? Or is the *best* you can do to give me a hug and tell me you're sorry so we know it won't happen again? Here's your lesson for today, Louie, and take it to the grave, because there's no better lesson in life but this...*Loyalty* breeds *friendship*, not the other way around. Cause you and me, we come in with the first beat of our hearts and leave when the heart stops beating...The *in-between* is about making sure that nobody influences who it beats *for*. Now, are you gonna fire that thing, or hug me?

1) This has a beginning, middle and end.

2) It's happening in the moment.

3) It's just between the two friends.

4) It is based on a physical threat and also life or death of a relationship.

5) It is founded in love.

6) It is three minutes or under.

Comedy—This might work well as a niche piece.

THE THINGAMAGIG

By Peter DeAnello

You've been going through my drawers, haven't you? Don't lie to me, Billy! I'm missing some things and one very important thing in particular…It's called a…"Thingamagig!" Yeah, that's it, a thingamagig…It is a special thingamagig that is very important to mommy…Well, it shakes when you twist the bottom and it looks like a rocket ship. Now, it's something that mommy doesn't want you to have…Show and what? Billy, what did you say about it in "Show and…?! I'm not yelling at you, but you have to remember, because…just because…Why couldn't you finish telling them about it? No, I've never seen a teacher laugh so hard to fall out of a chair…

Where is the thingamagig now? What Science contest? The library is a wonderful place to put the five finalists in…It just shakes, that's all…No, I don't know what happens when you mix baking soda with vinegar…Yes, you're very creative. Get your coat on now! Because we're going to the library and take home the thingamagig…I don't give a shit about a blue ribbon! You bet your little curious, thieving ass I'm yelling!

Don't cry. Mommy's sorry and didn't mean to curse. Forget the library, just pack a bag and mommy will too. We're moving to another town, another city, and probably another country, that's why! Mommy will buy you all the blue ribbons you want and paste them around your new room.

Billy, one more thing…What did you do with the little packages that were in the same drawer? You know, the ones…That's right, little rubber bubble things…Space suits for the astronauts…Why not? Of course that's a wonderful idea…Know what? Don't even worry about packing anything. Just get in the car. Now!

1) It has a beginning, middle and end.

2) It is happening in the moment.

3) It talks to one person until the teacher is mentioned.

4) Life or death? Not really, which is problematic. It is life or death of a reputation, but not between the two people in the scene.

5) The love foundation is important, so the mother is not just yelling at the son.

6) It is three minutes or under.

Dramedy—Irony about the future in relationship.

MARRY ME

By Peter DeAnello

Marry you? Of course I want to marry you. I've never known love like this.

It's not a question of whether I want to marry you. The question is whether you'll feel the same about me years from now. No, I'm not being silly. For once in my life, I'm being practical and not acting on a whim.

You've come into my life and I feel like I've finally found my soul mate. That's why I'm so afraid of you...Yes, because you could destroy me, in time. It's the irony of relationship. The person you love becomes the person you hate for the same reasons you love that person now. For who they are, in the depths of their soul, you'll later attack until the person fits into the mold called survival.

I know you don't understand that now. Think ahead. You love my creativity, right? You talk about hanging my paintings and sketches all over the house, but two years from now, you'll say, "Why don't you get a real job?" You love the fact that I work on my body, at least an hour in the gym every day. Soon, you'll tell me how self centered I am and vain. You love coming to watch me on stage. That will last as long as you get tired of two ships passing in the night during tech week.

Don't you see? We're in the infatuation stage of our relationship. I just don't want you to stop loving me. That's what I'm afraid of. If you love the artist in me, than you love the fact that I wear my heart on my sleeve. There's nothing guarding that heart. That's on purpose, but if I have to place that artist in a closet for the rest of my life, that will kill me just as much as if I came home one day and found a note and the side of your closet empty.

Yes, I'll marry you, but only after we honestly write down all the things we love about each other now. I need your promise that the list will hang over our bed for the rest of our lives, so we can remind ourselves when things get tough.

1) It has a beginning, middle and end.

2) It is happening in the moment.

3) It is just between the two people.

4) It is life or death of a relationship.

5) It is founded in love.

6) It is three minutes or under.

Farce—The zany sequel to Dr. Rightmind.

DR. RIGHTMIND—REVISITED

By Peter DeAnello

Dr. Rightmind, I don't honestly think that pipe up there will hold the weight of your body. You're so theatrical, but why don't you get off that desk now? C'mon, silly, I'm not going to bite you…today. At least, I don't think so. But, that's the thing about this oral fixation thing you discovered in me, I just get so excited that, well sometimes you just hurt the people you love. And, I pledge my love for you for the rest of my life.

You've got most of your bandages off. You know, I've read that vitamin E and aloe will take care of those unsightly bite scars. I'll rub that on you every night now. Hey, that reminds me!

I've got great news! I bought the house next to yours! Isn't that great? Now, you'll never be too far away from little old bite-size, me. I know you're a private guy and all, but I just couldn't help thinking that I would get to see you every day.

Oh, restraining orders are like candy…Every judge hands out at least one a day. They must have a quota or something. I'm so excited that you have a hot tub! I was just in your house. It wasn't hard. So why don't you come on down from there and let me give you a taste of what's ahead, for the rest of your life, you big lollipop!

1) It has a beginning, middle and end.

2) It's happening in the moment.

3) It's just between the two people.

4) It is the threat of physical death.

5) It is founded in a distorted love.

6) It is three minutes or under.

Drama—Love conquers all.

PATRICK

By Peter DeAnello

Patrick, I found your note, son. I'm glad you're still here. Before you pull that trigger, just hear me out, please. I know how you feel. It's amazing how stress and pressure make a person feel. It doesn't matter whether it's a job, life, or youth and peer pressure.

You can cry, it's alright, cause I'm right there with you. You know what I'm thinking? That I can go from being the luckiest parent in the world to the unluckiest as soon as you pull that trigger. I couldn't ask for a more loving, sensitive and intelligent child. That's what makes me so fortunate. If you pull that trigger, my life, my fortune changes forever. See, I can't end it, because I have you to live for and I know that we can survive anything together. You're *my* rock. Did you know that? I wake up every day and thank God for the most wonderful gift he could have ever blessed me with.

No, Please! Patrick, listen to one more thing. If you *have* to do that, I need you to just do one more thing before you do. If you're so sure that you want to end your life, grant me one wish before you do. Make that first bullet mine. Fire it right through my heart. If you don't, I'll die every day, over and over again, I promise you that. Every morning I'll wake up from this day forward and hear that gun shot and see, all over again, the last remnants of what was once my blessed son. I'll die with you, Patrick, but I'll do it more slowly and painfully. Or, I can wake up and keep thanking God and loving my life with my Boy. It's in your hands.

More pressure, huh? But, I promise we can face life together if you just take that pistol from your mouth. Is that a deal? (Sigh of relief) That's a good start, Patrick.

1) It has a beginning, middle and end.

2) It is happening in the moment.

3) It is just between the two people.

4) It is the threat of physical death. Ironically, it's also life or death of a relationship.

5) It is founded in love.

6) It is three minutes or under.

Drama—Military, but genderless.

THE MONSTERS

By Peter DeAnello

Hey little general, are you awake? I knew you would be. You wore those fatigue pajamas for me, didn't you? (Salutes) Reporting for deployment, sir. That was an excellent salute. You're the best little general that I've ever had the pleasure to serve under, sir.

Begging your pardon, but can I get a kiss goodbye? Yes, sir, because that kiss is going to have to last a long time. No, sir, I can't leave without that kiss. Because, there's no kiss like it in the world, never will be. There is no negotiating this point any longer, as I see it, sir. No, I *have* to collect that kiss, because I must fly out either way tonight. I've received my orders and they are to go fight the enemy to protect and serve you The enemy, sir? Well, they're the...monsters. I'll be in their country, fighting them, so they don't turn up here anymore, in your closet or under your bed. No monsters will be tolerated in our home or our country. I'll make sure of that, I promise.

Are you still negotiating that kiss, sir? Yes, I'll accept that challenge...I promise to return in trade for that kiss. Sir, you must promise that you will be good while I'm away and make sure all the military angels understand our promise every night during your prayers. I promise I will be saying the same prayers every night. Sir, tears will only stain both our uniforms...and you know what, that's just absolutely fine this evening. One more thing, could you add the biggest squeeze you've got to that kiss?

1) It has a beginning, middle and end.

2) It is happening in the moment.

3) It is talking with just one person.

4) It is life or death in this moment as it defines the future.

5) It is founded in love.

6) It is three minutes or under.

Comedy—Through irony. It's a coming of age twist on military and parenting.

SPECIAL OPS TRAINING

By Peter DeAnello

Straighten up for inspection! I'd just like to make myself clear about the next phase of your special training. You will rise at 0600 hours for the day, at which time you will proceed through the necessary physical and mental routine that has been established through your first five years at this base! However, due to your exceptional record for outstanding service to God, country, superior officers and dedication to your education and base duties up till this point, it is my distinct responsibility and pleasure to be the commanding officer that now leads you to your first major phase in special ops training. Understand that these orders are shared by me and the higher authority, who is currently...uh...crying behind that bedroom door!

In several minutes you will attend kindergarten for the first time and every day for several months. Each day, you will accompany your commanding officer on the one-quarter mile hike to this institution, holding his hand. It will commence with a kiss on the cheek before saluting with a wave, hug and squeeze of the hand. After said procedure, you will enter the special operations school.

You will be the ideal student and representative of this family and our nation. At no time will you lift your dress, pick your nose, put toys in your mouth, or throw things. You will never use your special forces training to pin, swat, or as a means of persuasive negotiation with any student and *especially* not your teacher...that is, unless otherwise provoked beyond measure. Is that understood?

You will share with others, nap at the appropriate time and respect everyone. At 12:00 hours, you will greet your father at the front of the school with a pressed handkerchief in hand to dry his eyes. At no time will you make fun of your blubbering dad because I will have missed my special ops baby. Do you have that handkerchief in possession at this time? Then, there is a change in orders. Please present it at this time?

1) It has a beginning, middle and end.

2) It is in the moment that she is about to start school.

3) It is talking with just one person, though the mother is mentioned.

4) Because it is not life or death as we have described, it suffers a bit.

5) It is founded in love.

6) It is three minutes or under.

Drama—Standing up to abuse.

THE ULTIMATUM

By Peter DeAnello

Mom, at the end of today, would you do me one favor? Will you look in the mirror and ask yourself, "Why did I drive my child out of the house?" Then, will you be honest with yourself?

See, I have to leave now, because I've decided that this is the last bruise I receive in our relationship. The reason I don't want you to ask that question of yourself now is because you're not sober enough to answer honestly.

You're a drunk and I can't live with that any longer. Tonight you'll either blame *me* for your problem or *yourself.* Then, decide to either get help or get drunk again. Welcome to bottom. I hope you crash hard, not to be mean, but to know that your next apology might actually mean something.

It's your turn to fight for me. If you don't, you won't see me again, because I'll know that you really do love the bottle more than me. It's an ultimatum, but it's all yours. If you think I'm doing this in spite…whatever it takes. Know what I've realized through all this? You can love your family, but you don't have to like them. I hope you make the right choice tonight, because it's lonely being me.

1) It has a beginning, middle and end.

2) It is happening in the moment.

3) It is just between the two people.

4) It is life or death of a relationship.

5) It is founded in love.

6) It is three minutes or under.

Drama—A what if, based on history.

THE PRESIDENT

By Peter DeAnello

Who was that just now? Do you have a woman in every city, John? I hoped this day would never come, that I would actually *find* you cheating on me. With all your human shields, I've only heard the whispers. But, if I can get through at a moment like this, maybe you better ride today in a protected motorcade?

After this ride today, we have to talk. The minute that motorcade exits Deeley Plaza, I want it driven back here so we can close the door. Then, I want an answer from you. Do we go on as husband and wife and no more cheating, or do I go on to Chicago or anywhere else for the rest of the campaign, dead inside, because my husband can't keep his zipper closed? But, I want a promise from you that either way, after today, we know whether we go on together or not.

I'm holding on by a thread, because the rest of me has died a little every day since you took office. The presidency has gone to your head, John. You're just a man—a very charismatic man, but just a man. And I've loved that man since forever and will forever again, but each infidelity has been a slap in my face. I believe this day will decide your fate. You have the Northern vote and this will only secure the South. That's why I need an answer by tonight. They'll have their president back, but I'm asking for my husband back. No matter what, I've never been in love with the position. I've been in love with the man. But if the man doesn't want me, then the president dies with him.

1) It has a beginning, middle and end.

2) It is happening in the moment.

3) It is just between the couple.

4) It is life or death of a relationship.

5) It is founded in love.

6) It is three minutes or under.

Comedy—Be careful what you ask for.

THE HEAT OF PASSION

By Peter DeAnello

I'm home! Why the look of surprise? You asked me to move in and I'm home. I have a three-time rule during the heat of passion. (Imitating him) "Oh, ooh! OOOHHHH! Move in! Marry Me! Move in! MARRY ME! MOVE IN, DAM-NIT!" The way I see it is, once means you're in throes of imagination. Twice means you're considering the possibilities. Third time's a charm! One more "Marry me, damnit!" and I'll set the date.

Now, this is only the first load of my things. The way I figure it, there are thirty-three or so more truckloads. I'm going to like it here. There's only one thing, though...Some of your things are going to have to go. I'm a bit of a pack rat, and I kind of *collect* things, like dolls, spoons, arrowheads, Disney memorabilia, and cats...eighteen to date. I'm very clean, though. They're going to love you. There's so much here for them to perch on...beds, leather furniture, counter tops and tables...Did you know that cats are the cleanest animals?

So, the way I see it, there's a decision to be made at this moment, or forever hold your tongue. You can either help me move in, at which time you get a say so in where things go, and what of yours may or may not stay-Or, I'll be happy to do it all if you want to go and watch that football game at the corner bar. But on your way home, you might want to stop at the pet store and buy a dozen or so scratch-ing posts, three hundred pounds of litter and five cases of Science Diet.

This is so great! As soon as I'm moved in, we can make love all night, every night! You know what I love most about you? I've never been with anyone so talkative during sex. Don't ever change that.

1) It has a beginning, middle and end.

2) It is happening in the moment.

3) It is just between the two people.

4) It may not necessarily be life or death of a relationship, but it does establish the boundaries of a new one.

5) It is founded in passion, not love.

6) It is three minutes or under.

Drama—One to tug on the heartstrings.

THE DREAM IS BIG ENOUGH, SO...

By Peter DeAnello

Hey there. How do you feel about spending the rest of your life with me? Let's see, here are the requirements...I come with a real need to be loved and hugged on...I require an infinite number of kisses every day, and if you can find it in your heart to call me daddy (mommy) at least once a day, you'll melt my very soul for the rest of my life.

I don't know why you were in such a hurry to enter this world, but I want to hear all about it some day. Right now, we need to talk about the reasons to stick around. See, all that can be done to keep you here, has been done. The rest is up to you.

All I have right now is a need to hug and kiss my angel and a few promises. If you stick around, I promise you'll never know a day without my arms around you to warm you, or my kisses to seal our love. You'll never know a day without my smile to encourage your dreams. I'll make every day Christmas because I promise every day to give all that I have to you. That's my gift, the gift of unconditional love. If that's a good reason for you to stay, then you fight as hard as you can. I'm going to write something next to your name on this bassinet, if that's alright with you. I'm going to write, "Michael, Louis...My dream is big enough, so the facts don't count." And when you open your eyes for the first time, you'll see me.

   1) It has a beginning, middle and end.

   2) It is happening in the moment.

   3) It is just between the two people.

   4) It is the threat of physical death, as well as life or death of a relationship.

   5) It is founded in love.

   6) It is three minutes or under.

Comedy—Survival of the fittest.

ONE, TWO, THREE...SHOOT!

By Peter DeAnello

You almost drowned me back there! You pulled me under! You did too! It's not enough you're a better swimmer than me, you didn't have to fight dirty. OK, OK, if it's down to just us, let's just catch our breath before we go on? Frankly, you don't deserve to win for fighting dirty. That's bad Karma, not to mention bad sportsmanship. Look, if someone has to lose and someone has to win, I'm OK with that, but let's at least do it in a civilized fashion, fair enough? Let's...Uh...choose! Why not? The best two out of three wins. Let's shoot for it. C'mon, odds and evens. Ready? One, two, three...shoot!

(He/she puts out two fingers and loses) Alright, one for you. One, two, three...shoot! (Loses again). Cut that out! (A deep breath) One, two three, shoot! (Wins) AHAA! (A deep breath) One, two three...shoot! (Wins again) Yes! OK, so we're at a tie. This is crazy, isn't it? Ready? Why are you crying? The odds are in your favor! You're the one who was trying to drown me a second ago. Now, tears? I can do without you crying. Look at us. Talk about a million to one odds?

OK. Ready? One, two...Wait! (Hyperventilating) This is beautiful, you're crying and I'm having an anxiety attack. Let's breathe, OK? Thank you. You know, you're not half bad when not you're not trying to murder me, the first thing you do in life. Thank you, and I want you to know that no matter who wins, I appreciate your cooperation. I'm really a pacifist.

Ready? One, two...Wait a minute...Look, I didn't mind the punching, biting and scratching to get here. That's survival. But, you're not so bad. This is crazy. Time is running out for either of us, so let's get on with it...Huh?...Both of us? You mean, as in we both get in? (Considers it) I mean, it will get a little tight and all, but what the heck, it's only for nine months! At least we both win...Just promise, no more dirty fighting, ever...Deal?

1) It has a beginning, middle and end.

2) It's happening in the moment.

3) It is just between them.

4) It's the threat of physical death.

5) Love is being developed as the piece develops.

6) It's three minutes or under.

Drama—Ultimatums are a great tool in deciding life or death situations.

THE CHOICE

By Peter DeAnello

You know what, Steve? This date is starting to get out of hand. I'm becoming a little concerned about our future. Please hear me. I don't want this to go any further than it has. Do you understand that? Neither one of us needs to drink any more than we have, and you need to understand that what comes next will be a new beginning for us. It's in your hands. You have two choices and both start the same way, but have different endings.

Either way, I know it will begin with me staring at your yearbook picture tomorrow morning. Option one will end with praying that you call me again. I'll dream about a nice dinner, movie and spending more time with you. That will mean that you finished the evening with compassion, understanding and control tonight.

Option two starts the day with your yearbook picture in a police report. That's a promise, because I don't believe in mistakes. I won't look back at this and forgive a mistake. See, a mistake is accidentally bumping into a table and knocking over a glass of milk. Tonight is about a choice. I choose to stop, now.

Now, it's your turn to choose, but before you decide, can I tell you what I've been dreaming about? I'd love to be at your next baseball game, and every one after that, cheering for my boyfriend. I'd love to look in the stands during my volleyball games and see you. I'd love to celebrate birthdays together and be under the mistletoe with only you at Christmas.

Which option are you going to choose, Steve? I have a volleyball game tomorrow night. Would you like to be there?

1) It has a beginning, middle and end.

2) It is happening in the moment.

3) It is just between the two people.

4) It is life or death of a relationship.

5) It is founded in love.

6) It is three minutes or under.

Comedy—Coming of age.

THE ROCKET SHIP

By Peter DeAnello

Intercourse? What are you asking me about that for? It's a town in Pennsylvania. I'm serious! Look, why don't you wait four years until you're sixteen? By then, I'll have a nice lady in my life by then and you can ask her. What are they teaching you in school, anyway? This is not important at this moment in time. By the way, how was band practice? I'm not changing the subject!

OK, it's the *course* of action someone takes when *inter...*facing with a new program. OK, OK! Get a pad and paper. Draw a rocket ship. That's a very *generous* rocket ship. Get another piece of paper. Because, I don't want you thinking that all rocket ships are that big! That's not a normal rocket ship. As a matter of fact, if you *ever* see one that big, just run! Alright, fine, draw a tunnel just a bit too small for the rocket ship to pass through...No, it's not silly, it's *ridiculous*! Isn't your teacher a female? Don't you have health class?

Fine, fine, what do you think happens when the rocket ship tries to enter the tunnel? Exactly! It won't fit! So the moral of the story is: don't even try! Now, how was band practice?

Come back here...Clarity? You want clarity, try the library or talk to your grandmother about this. OK! When two people fall in love, they engage...perform...they just get naked and get it on, OK? Are you happy now? I'm not good at the particulars. It's a natural act...That's what *who* said? Who's *he*? Aright, YOU WANT CLARITY? You call him and get him over here right now and I'll get real clear about things! It's amazing how clear I'm feeling now! Clarity is suddenly my middle name! Call him. Then, while we wait for "Mr. Natural," next to that rocket ship, draw a picture of a gun, A VERY LARGE GUN! Is that clear?!

1) It has a beginning, middle and end.

2) It is happening in the moment.

3) It mentions others. This is where it falls short a bit.

4) It only becomes life or death when the threat of a gun is mentioned.

5) It is founded in love.

6) It is three minutes or under.

Comedy—Irony used to build armor.

BULLETPROOF

By Peter DeAnello

OK, let's get this over with, because I have a feeling you'll stick around and that's not good for either of us...Because, I'm at the end of my emotional rope! Why can't you get the message?

One more time...Ready? You're goofy, silly, and I don't even like you. I wouldn't marry you if you were the last person in the world, let alone ask you out on a date. If we were stranded on a desert island, I'd find a sharp shell and slit my wrists. If I could find a poison plant I'd eat the whole thing. If there were a ferocious animal there, I'd stick my whole head in its mouth, rather than spend a minute more there with you!

Why are you still here? Need more? Your nose is crooked and nothing matches on your face. The angels who tried to match your ears never had their eyes checked, and speaking of your eyes, they seem to be closer than the closest of friends. Furthermore, if you blow-dry your hair one more time, grazing cows will think it's dinnertime! Heaven knows that, on the Richter Scale, your looks could sink a continent. And, I mean all that in the nicest way.

However, you are kind, considerate and trustworthy. You're honest, to a fault, and animals love you. You are a *decent* cook, you're neat and floss every day. Fortunately, I don't trust anyone, never have. Kind people usually have ulterior motives, I don't need a cook, I have a maid, and the floss thing grosses me out. So let me lift my shoe and you can pick up your heart and run along with what's left of it.

(A deep sigh. He/she checks the mirror and smiles) There, now you're bullet proof. Let's see anyone beat that? I still love you!

1) It has a beginning, middle and end.

2) It is happening in the moment.

3) It is talking to just one person.

4) It is life or death of an emotion.

5) It is founded in an ironic form of love.

6) It is three minutes or under.

Comedy—For women only (sorry guys).

THE STICK

By Peter DeAnello

Go ahead and run me over! I won't blame you. But, just listen first? Please? Just roll the window down. I promise I won't punch, kick, scratch or slap. Just an inch, so I won't have to shout. It's been a rough month, huh? OK, six weeks…And two days…And three hours…And twenty-three minutes. Fine, are you finished? Look, I paid all the doctor bills, didn't I? I'm kidding, Rob. It was a joke…A bad one.

I love you. I said it, alright? And, if you leave, I'll be lost and depressed. I won't have anyone to eat Haagen-Dazs with at three am. I just want to show you one thing, alright? If you go after that, I'll understand. It's in the house. No, I won't bring it out. You have to come in. It's a stick, alright?! What is there to be afraid of? I'm a hundred and five pounds soaking wet. You're my two hundred and fifty-pound muscle bound teddy bear.

Roll the window down again! It's not a stick to beat you with! I promise. I threw out the frying pan, the bat, the rest of the dishes, even the frozen chicken. They're in the trash. Look for yourself. No, I'm not going to bring it over here and show you. What do you want me to do, itemize every household weapon on the hood of the car? There's not a single projectile left in the house, I promise, unless you count paper plates and plastic forks. We don't own a gun that I'm aware of, and I don't even touch the kitchen knives…at least when you're awake. Will you relax? I'm joking!

C'mon…Pookey…Schnookums…Stud-muffin…Now, don't you feel better? The stick? It is about three inches long and it has lines on it. Today it has two lines! That's what makes it wonderful, the second line! It explains why my temper has been so out of control. Want the good news now? My temper problem is only going to last another nine months! (He faints) Rob? Get up! Can you hear me? Damnit, now you're going to think I hit you again when you wake up!

1) It has a beginning, middle and end.

2) It is happening in the moment.

3) It is just between the two people.

4) It is life or death of a relationship, along with the threat of physical harm.

5) It is founded in love.

6) It is three minutes or under.

Drama—Could be about a son, brother, best friend, etc. You decide.

THE CLEANER

By Peter DeAnello

Do you know what I really do for a living, Joe? I'm a cleaner. What does that mean to you? Right, I'm a janitor...of sorts. I know you've always been embarrassed by that. You're right to feel that way, but you don't know why. I clean other people's messes. I clean them so well that no one knows a mess ever existed in the first place.

I've placed on the table all my cleaning tools. There's a hatchet, a saw, a cleaver, plenty of rags, trash bags, hospital masks, the most powerful carpet cleaner and wet/dry vacuum money can buy. There's a host of chemicals that, when used full strength, can remove bloodstains from any porous material, and melt iron if necessary. It's all about not leaving a trace.

I'm supposed to clean a mess in this apartment in a few hours. There will be blood everywhere, probably even on the ceiling. I promise it will either be yours or mine...better that it's mine. It's amazing what happens when a knife, an axe, a bullet pierces the body.

You've got a problem and I can't fix it anymore, son. Knowing that I'm risking my life by coming here now, I'm begging you to disappear forever. My life savings, thirty-five gees, is under your hat on the table. Take it, walk out the back door, and never look back. Change your identity and don't ever go into a card room, a racetrack, or borrow money again. Don't be seen in Vegas or Atlantic City, and don't ever call me again or anyone you know here.

Or, the next time I see you again, it will be when I'm dividing my own son into trash bags and dumping you all over the city. I lose you either way, today. That's my tragedy, but I don't want to piece you up like a butcher in a meat plant.

1) It has a beginning, middle and end.

2) It is happening in the moment.

3) It is between just the two people.

4) It is life or death of a relationship and the threat of physical death.

5) It is founded in love.

6) It is three minutes or under.

Comedy—Irony in the battle of the sexes.

FELIX

By Peter DeAnello

I've taken the liberty to wash, press, fold your clothes and pack your bags. They're by the door and the keys to my car are sitting on top of the signed title to the vehicle. It's washed, polished and vacuumed. The oil has been changed and I included a fresh box of tissues on the console (just in case you'll miss me as much as I'll miss you), next to a new toothbrush, tube of toothpaste and floss for the trip. I want to thank you for a wonderful time, but I feel that if I spend seven more days with you, I'll drive you crazy.

Look, I fold my underwear, separate my vitamins and my CD's and books are meticulously shelved in alphabetical order. I don't smoke, I prefer cats to dogs, because they're cleaner, and I can't sit down to eat until the pots, stove and cooking utensils are cleaned first.

In a few days you'll begin to refer to me as "Felix," call me "obsessive," and wonder (in secret, if not out loud) whether I prefer partners of the same sex. "Why can't he just be like the other guys?" Why can't I just burp, fart and scratch in public? It's not me and I don't see the need to change for anyone or do anything just because it's accepted behavior in bars and locker rooms.

But, before you leave, Susan, I just want to say that you are the greatest thing that's ever happened to me. Your veal picatta is to die for! I now know positions I never knew existed, and you're the first woman I've ever been with who puts the toilet seat down without my constant prodding. You take good care of your teeth, body and hair...Huh? What's wrong with the way I set my slippers? They look straight to me...(smiles) But then, nobody's perfect...Maybe you can stay just a little bit longer?

    1) It has a beginning, middle and end.

    2) It is happening in the moment.

3) It is just between the two people.

4) It is life or death of a relationship.

5) It is founded in love.

6) It is three minutes or under.

Black Comedy—With shades of gray.

THE LAMP

By Peter DeAnello

That's not a rifle, it's the...uh...stem of a lamp. Where is that darn shade? I've been meaning to replace it...don't pull the trigger! And, point it down, will you please? I know your rule about no guns. I just have it around for protection. You never know who will just come in and...steal you! I would just die if anyone stole you. It's not that I can just go to the store and buy another you. You're one of a kind, one in a million, my one and...List of names? Just people I need to...confront...(Jumps in the air to avoid a bullet to the foot) Are you crazy?! Put the safety back on that thing. Yes, your name is on that list too! It's crossed out, or haven't you noticed that? (He jumps up again to avoid another bullet to the foot) Because, I fell in love with you, that's why! Will you please just stop for one second?

Thank you! What are you, a saint? You assassinate with words. That's the only difference between us. What's worse, to physically destroy one time or inflict emotional and psychological pain every day? That's what you do! You pull the trigger every day on articles against very "colorful" individuals. You've stopped doing that, or haven't you noticed?

That's a very healthy thing, because prison walls don't stop orders from being given or carried out. I made a promise that no more would be written. I put *my life* on the line for you with that promise! Because since I've met you, I haven't fired that thing once. I have a reason not to assassinate anymore. Because of you, I stopped hating myself.

Because, since you, the purpose I get up in the morning has changed. Hey, I've noticed you haven't been bashing people lately in your articles. So, if it's OK with you, that gun really would make a nice lamp. I just have to find the right shade…Bedside would be great…my side…Just in case anyone tries to steal you in the middle of the night.

1) It has a beginning, middle and end.

2) It is happening in the moment.

3) It is just between the two people, though others are suggested.

4) It is threat of physical death.

5) It is founded in love.

6) It is three minutes and under.

Comedy—Through Metaphors.

TWICE FALLEN

By Peter DeAnello

Did I just hear that correctly? You want me to propose to you while bungee jumping the Grand Canyon? Are you nuts?! Don't answer that. You'll burst whatever illusion I have left. What's better than that? Underwater, surrounded by sharks, in a whale's stomach would be better. At the mouth of an active volcano, on the street during the bull-run in Spain, blindfolded in front of a firing squad. That's better. While riding the cyclone at Coney Island, in the lion's cage at the zoo during feeding time, or in the yard of a maximum security prison during recess.

Why do you want an answer now? Reserve what? Look, just give me something to stand on or hold onto. Yes, heights are what I'm most terrified of! I get n se-bleeds changing a light bulb on a six-foot ladder. (Stops) OK, I get it. Cle er. You had me worried. Metaphors! Fine…OK, I can embrace a metaphor.

Look, I'm not going anywhere, OK? When the going gets tough, I'll be reaching for my Bible instead of the car keys. On our wedding day, my ring gets super glued to my finger and the biggest strip of Velcro to my hip.

You're nodding. That's good…positive…understandable. I'm following your lead. Metaphors are healthy in a relationship. I can appreciate the need and use for them now. You scared me there for a second. What are you doing with that stretchy rope? Yes, it's a very nice rope…very long. That's a very nice map. (Reading) "The Grand Canyon" I guess when I say I do, I'll have fallen for you…twice.

1) It has a beginning, middle and end.

2) It is happening in the moment of decision.

3) It is happening just between the two people.

4) It is life or death of a relationship and the threat of physical death, but not in the moment.

5) It is founded in love.

6) It is three minutes or under.

Comedy—Fleshing out a problem.

VULNERABLE

By Peter DeAnello

Look, I'm thinking maybe I shouldn't refer to you as "Shorty" anymore, or, "The little woman"…or "Tid-bit." I know, it's just a name, but silly little things like nick names can offend people and sometimes make them do other silly little things like pull a loaded weapon on someone when they are minding their own business, sitting on the office toilet. But, let's not talk about the obvious right now. This looks like an excellent time to talk about a raise, profit sharing, or that partnership in the firm.

Squirming? Of course I'm squirming. I have diarrhea and my secretary, excuse me, partner, is holding a gun on me, with no relief for either in sight. *Squirming* seems to be the way to go at the moment. Ouch! No, of course you didn't do anything…But, I appreciate the burst of compassion at the moment. That was the crab I ate last night. I accidentally swallowed a shell. I'm alright, yes I am. I'm just fine now. I'm a little less embarrassed that it's you holding the gun and not anyone else. No, of course there's no one else that would hold a gun on me in the executive toilet. But, all in all, I am somewhat happier and in some ways healthier, thank you very much for asking.

Yes, that is a *woman's* phone number on my PalmPilot. I have a lot of phone numbers in my palm pilot, and I do business with women. Well, it's come up a lot because I've called it a lot. No, thank you for the directness of the question, but I'm not cheating on you. I'm cheating *with* you. I'm married *to* you. I thought we agreed that we would play that game between home and the office, so we never feel the need to play another with anyone else? We agreed that you would be a little less jealous if we played that game…Yaaaooooo! No, that was probably another clamshell…and, possibly also my heart breaking. It hurts that you would question me with an unfounded accusation; especially at this vulnera-

ble time…I love you too. Please close the door. Thank you. Ah! No, "shor—"
Dear. I don't know what that was, but I'm glad it's over.

1) It has a beginning, middle and end.

2) It is happening in the moment.

3) It is just between the two people, though another woman is mentioned.

4) It is life or death of a relationship and the threat of physical death.

5) It is founded in love.

6) It is three minutes or under.

Drama—In metaphors.

THINGS

By Peter DeAnello

Sweetie, have you seen my heart? I seem to have…oh, there it is, under your foot. I can tell it's mine, because it has been ripped out of my chest very recently. Could you hand me that spatula, please, so I can scoop it up and return what's left of it where it belongs? I realize that to you it's just another *thing*, but I kind of need it, you know, to start breathing again. But, don't let me interrupt you any further with what you were doing.

Speaking of *things*, I seem to be just frozen here in the kitchen, trying to settle some of them in my mind. It's not every day I come home and find my bed busy with activity and only one of us is part of the activity. But, that's no longer the issue for me. What amazes me now, as I look around, is that all these things were happy reminders in our life a few minutes ago. In a single moment, they've all turned against me. So, I realize that I need to say goodbye to them. Not for what they are but for what they represent.

What I'm going to do is leave you everything. I've signed over the cars in your maiden name and the titles are on the table. I feel a little better that this *thing* issue has been settled. Thank you for all of them. They served a wonderful purpose.

1) It has a beginning, middle and end.

2) It is happening in the moment.

3) It is just between the two people.

4) It is life or death of a relationship

5) It is founded in love.

6) It is three minutes or under.

Dramedy—Making lemonade.

A WALK IN THE PARK

By Peter DeAnello

(Seated perfectly still) I…uh…I'm not ready to come home today. I need you to understand that, OK? I don't know how much longer, but I just can't come home now. Hey, what are you crying for? Look, I sat up all by myself. I'm going to be walking again in no time, you'll see. It will be soon, but not today. This accident thing, it's a walk in the park. But, I need to start doing some more things by myself before I come home. You're going to think the accident affected my brain too, when I tell you why.

I made myself a promise a long time ago that I would never go to a female doctor. I want you to always see your husband through the eyes of *Mrs.* Filbin, not *Dr.* Filbin. Think about it. You've seen me naked, but under very different circumstances, don't you agree? In the future, when we make love, am I just going to be a clinical specimen to you or will I still turn you on? Are you going to make love to me, thinking, "I wonder how his prostate is doing?" Why don't I just check and see?" Or, in the middle of a climactic moment, will you ask me to cough?

Today, its "I love you, let's make love." I don't want tomorrow to be, "Do you have a scheduled appointment to make love with your wife?" or "Please fill out this brief history of our encounters and sexual history." I realize you could sign me out and take me home, regardless of how I feel, and I won't be able to do a thing about it. But, I'm begging you to let me keep what's left of my dignity just a little bit longer?

That's the smile I love. Every day, I feel things I haven't the day before. Today, I felt myself breathing for the first time again. See, I'll be home in no time. Like I said, it's a walk in the park.

1) It has a beginning, middle and end.

2) It is happening in the moment.

3) It is just between the two people.

4) It is life or death of an emotion in that he wants to keep his dignity in the relationship.

5) It is founded in love.

6) It is three minutes or under.

Drama—An example of how the threat of physical death could result in the death of a relationship.

RHYTHM

By Peter DeAnello

Wake up, you sleepyhead. Good morning. I wanted a few moments with you before I'm wheeled out of here. You know, it's a crime what we take for granted in our lives. This is the first time in my life that I watched the sunrise from start to finish. It's so perfect and natural.

I woke before the sunrise and found us nose to nose and I realized that the rhythm of our breathing was perfectly synchronized. I never realized before that we must adapt the same breathing rhythm while sleeping. A little Divine joke, huh? Most people never realize that the time when they are most in rhythm with their partner is when they are least aware of it. So perfect and so natural, just like that sunrise that we also take for granted. That gave me hope through this. I've asked for a sign in my prayers that I'll wake up and with you again. I think this is it.

I'm going to make sure that the last thought I think, as the anesthesia is putting me out, is how perfect we are together—how the most natural thing in my life is that we should never be apart-that we should wake up every day and know that we are in rhythm, from each beat of our hearts to every breath we take.

I may look funny after today, for a while, but we'll laugh about it in the light of every sunrise from this day on. Promise me you'll think those thoughts with me as my eyes close, and that you'll be the first sight I see when they open again. And, there's nothing to worry about, right?

1) It has a beginning, middle and end.

2) It is happening in the moment.

3) It is just between the two people.

4) It is life or death of a relationship due to the threat of physical death.

5) It is founded in love.

6) It is three minutes or under.

Comedy—With ulterior motives.

RECENTLY SINGLE

By Peter DeAnello

(She is seated, gripping the chair tightly with both hands) I know we don't know each other, but you had a really calming voice when you said hello. I need *calm* right now. See, it's my first time in one of these things and it seems to be about to go down. How ironic is that? I knew it would. I mean, I'm not psychic or anything, at least not seeing dead people. Although, it looks like in a few moments we're about to see plenty of them. (Gripping tighter—gasps) This is just turbulence, right? Very *bad* turbulence!

(It steadies again) That's better. You must be a great husband to someone special, but I'm feeling like if you're the last person I see in life, I should at least know your name. Peter. That's is a nice name. It's a strong name. Biblical. I wonder if that counts for anything up there? It means *rock*, right? See, I know my Bible. Maybe that counts too, you know when we're being judged and all? Think so? Thank you for agreeing. You're polite, too.

You're a good man. I can tell. I hope you have someone who appreciates that. Recently single too, huh? Well, then maybe you won't mind holding me? I'm just thinking that maybe it might ease things on the way down or when it reaches the ground. (Turbulence) Ahhh! I love you!

OK, it's leveled off again. I'm sorry for that outburst. But what the heck, right? I've been admiring you since you sat next to me. When you reached down to get your seat belt and accidentally touched me, I admit that I was (turbulence) excited! Who the *hell* is driving this thing?

Sorry, bad choice of words, huh? I'm sorry, again, Peter. Catholic? Jewish. That's probably a better faith to be at this moment in time. I feel safer now. I'm sure most of Heaven is of that faith, or at least much of the influential part. Hey, if we get separated, will you look for me? (Turbulence) Ohhh, we're going down! Huh? Yes! I'm free every night! I hate roller coasters!

1) It has a beginning, middle and end.

2) It is happening in the moment.

3) It is talking to just one person.

4) It is founded in a strong attraction...Love? Maybe in the moment.

5) It is life or death of a relationship and the illusion of physical death.

6) It is three minutes and under.

Drama—How about a love story, also with the use of Irony.

THE TOTAL PACKAGE

By Peter DeAnello

(He is stuttering badly) I know I'm probably not doing this the best way, but please don't say anything until I finish…Thanks for playing along for a moment. I'm nervous enough…(He starts to lose the stuttering, as he takes her hand in his and lowers to one knee) See, the sweet sound of your voice seems to reach down and take my breath away. My heart seems to disconnect from my head and my mouth. (Without realizing it, he loses the stutter completely).

You've never known how the sight of you melts me. When you walk by, I swear time stops. I've never known the feeling of complete joy for just being near you or the pounding of my heart each time we kiss…I've loved you forever and will forever again.

You are the total package of the vision I hoped and prayed actually existed for me. I know that if you say yes, I'll cherish every moment of every hour for the rest of our lives together…

(He fumbles to find the ring and suddenly realizes that this is the moment of truth and begins stuttering again.) So, I want to ask…(He can't stop stuttering and suddenly struggles to put the words together. He stops.) You're nodding. (He nods *yes* with her)…Yes?! Is that a yes? So you will…and we'll be…and forever you and me? The total package!

1) It has a beginning, middle and end.

2) It is happening in the moment.

3) It is just between the two lovers.

4) It is life or death of a relationship.

5) It is founded in love.

6) It is three minutes or under

Drama—Irony in choice.

WELCOME BACK

By Peter DeAnello

I hear you were released today on good behavior. Congratulations. I wanted to be the first to welcome you back to society. Sounds like your therapy has been more effective than mine. See, I couldn't get you off my mind the past few years. I'm still in love with you, even after only one night. Even though, you'll probably rape again...I hope you realize that fact.

See, I've been trying to stop killing for years. As hard as I've tried, I just can't seem to stop. The only difference between us is that I just haven't gotten caught. So, do we play *hide and seek*, or do I put a bullet in your head now? I'm sorry, I fell in love with you, but there's just no room for anyone else in my life. You understand that, don't you? But, because I love you, I'm going to offer *you* a running start.

I thought about putting a bullet in your head right now, but the idea of losing you all at once will be too painful for me. That's fair, isn't it? If I destroy you, one piece at a time, somehow I believe I can deal with the loss more easily.

First, my car bumper will find your knees at the curb of a busy intersection. Next, never put your drink down at bars or parties to find your next victim the way you found me...the lining in your stomach will never mend. Don't even think about getting into your car without checking the back seat, or take a leisurely walk or lounge on your porch...for the rest of your life.

Finally, I found the store that carried the same knife you seem to like to use in your exploits. It's going to be with that knife that I separate you from your weapon and watch you bleed to death. Did you know that in Medieval times most people didn't die from the knife or sword wound, but from the animal feces they stabbed their weapon in before the battle? How sad is it that we're so right for each other, but that your therapy was so much more successful than mine? So, in closing, I'll give you thirty seconds to decide. What's it going to be, now or later?

1) It has a beginning, middle and end.

2) It is happening in the moment, though it is based on the past.

3) It is just between the two people.

4) It is the threat of physical death.

5) It's based on a very distorted love.

6) It is three minutes or under.

Drama—How young love blossoms!

HYPOTHETICAL LOVE

By Peter DeAnello

Great job. I hate closing a show, don't you? "Hypothetical Love," what a great name for a play, huh? It was fun being *hypothetically* in love with you. Hey, I don't know how to get in touch with you. I mean, *hypothetically*, if we did another scene again, we could maybe work on another one like this, since we work so well together. No, I don't have the scene yet. But, *hypothetically*, it might pick up where this one left off. It might take place in a five star restaurant, instead of just a café, and the two lovers…us…Maybe we could research the roles in a really romantic way.

How? Well, I'll pick you up in a limo. I'll be holding a corsage. Of course, this time I'll be wearing a tux instead of just a suit and tie. You'll be wearing your best formal gown, instead of a business suit, your hair flowing over your shoulders, instead of pulled back.

I'll rent out the whole restaurant for the evening, so it's just the two of us. The blazing fire in the large brick fireplace will be the only light in the room, except for the single candle on our table, next to the ceiling-to-floor picture window that overlooks the snow-capped mountains. Before dinner we'll dance to an orchestra, instead of a jukebox.

After dessert, the limo will drive us to the most romantic spot, overlooking the city. We'll toast the full moon with expensive champagne in crystal glasses, instead of glass. We'll dance without any accompaniment, and not even realize it. Then, I'll see you home. Then? I don't know for sure, I'm not a writer, but maybe we could write the rest of this script together? We can continue where the last script left off, *hypothetically* speaking…Right now is just fine. I'll get my things.

1) It has a beginning, middle and end.

2) It is happening in the moment.

3) It is just between the two people.

4) It is life or death of a relationship, since they may never see each other again.

5) It is founded in a deep attraction to each other.

6) It is three minutes or under.

Comedy—The things we do for love.

YOU FIRST

By Peter DeAnello

What are you doing out here? Are you nuts? It's a long way down. You'll fall and break your neck! Yeah, well, could you pick another time? What do you think I was doing? Praying to God for the strength to go ahead with it. Anyway, I was out here first, which means that I get to go first. Way to go, cutting in line, the last thing you do in life.

Why shouldn't I jump? What do you care? Look at you, two seconds away from jumping, too. Get back together with you? I'll be afraid you'll take a dive while I'm at work some day.

Know what, I've changed my mind. You go first. Because, you might see me splat and think twice about it, then tomorrow you'll fall in love again and I'll have a bird's eye view of it all. That's why.

Yes, I love you! What the hell do you think I'm doing up here? I've been waiting for you. Because if I would have heard you talk about jumping one more time in your sleep, I would go nuts. Besides that, your diary had this day and time written in it…Why not, our anniversary is just as good a time as any.

Of course I don't really want to kill myself! I've been waiting up here, freezing, for the past hour because I thought you might rush things…I'm saying it now. I love you, damnit! No, I didn't say damnit because I'm sorry I love you, I said it because I'm afraid of heights! If I tell you every day from now on, and wake you with kisses and hugs, and come home with a single rose in the evening, then will you stay grounded? Well, I didn't know until I read it in the diary. Can we please go in now? See how easy that was? Just do me one favor? Toss the diary and talk to me when you want something, so I don't have to do this anymore, OK? Thank you.

1) It has a beginning, middle and end.

2) It is happening in the moment.

3) It is just between the couple.

4) It is life or death of a relationship and the threat of physical death.

5) It is founded in love.

6) It is three minutes or under.

Comedy—The irony of lying to keep a relationship together.

LIE

By Peter DeAnello

My bag is packed because I'm leaving you. Have you ever thought that I might want to just have one personal thought and keep it to myself? I mean mystery is a good thing, don't you think? Falling in love with a psychic really has its challenges, doesn't it? OK, so I was going to say "problems," but I thought "challenges" would sound better, you know? Cut that out!

No, I don't really want to leave! Of course you know that. Why did I even pack the bag? I packed...for effect, OK? I wanted you to realize how serious this is getting. Drama isn't necessarily bad in a relationship. It creates anticipation. Anticipation is good. Mystery is good. I feel like I'm connected to a lie detector test around you. You tell me what I'm feeling, when I'm feeling it, even before I'm feeling it! My thoughts have become about measuring my thoughts.

You already know that I love you and that I don't want anyone else and that I'm mostly normal...I think. But, that doesn't matter either because you think what I think, since I'm thinking it. I don't think that's healthy. I mean for you it is, but for me to be thinking about what you're thinking that I'm thinking. I want to be able to surprise you with what I think...I think. I think I'm going nuts! I hope you'll love me in white, because that's the color of the jacket I'll be in. It will be made of canvas and have long arms, with leather straps.

No, I wasn't thinking that. I was thinking that the worst part of being committed would be being away from you. Yes, I was! (A beat) Are you serious? You didn't know I was thinking that? Really? Wait a minute...(To himself) Was I really thinking that? Yes I was, I know I was. I also know you're a bad liar, but you lied because you love me, didn't you? Can you lie a little more? It would make me feel a little less naked, you know? Promise? Is that a lie or the truth? Listen, if you can lie, or maybe just not tell me what I'm thinking all the time, I might not need that jacket with the long arms, you know? Of course I love you. I was just about to tell you that. Cut it out!

1) It has a beginning, middle and end.

2) It is happening in the moment.

3) It is just between the couple.

4) It is life or death of a relationship.

5) It is founded in love.

6) It is three minutes or under.

Farce—With a twist.

BRO

By Peter DeAnello

Bro, what the hell are you doing six hundred miles into the war zone, on my ship? I joined the Navy to get away from you and, suddenly it's not far enough! Miss you? I don't even like you. We're only half brothers and you're the wacko half! Now, get out of here. Go. Shoo! I get it now. This is a dream, a nightmare.

You're not real and I'm going to wake up and embrace this godforsaken place because anywhere is better than being home, victim to your pranks. You know what the best part of this war is for me? I just have to worry about dying *one time*! I'm not lighting cigarettes and having them blow up in my face, or finding itching powder in my bed, or black widow spiders in my shoes, or pet rattlesnakes under my pillow. I'm no longer checking my mail for letter bombs. Knives don't suddenly stick to the door next to my head as I leave a room. I'm not checking for rats in the toilet when I get up to pee at night.

You're a lunatic! You should have been committed years ago. Look at you. You look like hell! What are you talking about, buried today? I thought the snake was your favorite pet. Why would it bite you? I told you to stop kissing that snake. Of course it pissed him off. Gone, huh? Wow. So, this is like more than a dream? (He sits, depressed) You mean, I joined this war for nothing? Go figure...

I'm kidding, stop crying. Of course I'm feeling bad...Because, I've been missing you. Yeah, you're a pinhead, but you never lied to me and I can handle almost anything today because of you. You taught me to have eyes in the back of my head and I can sleep with one eye open. As much as I hate to admit it, those things come in handy here.

I can't believe I'm saying this, but I appreciate all you did. What do you mean, you've gotta go? You just got here…Yeah, sure…Take care…Yeah, see ya when I see ya, bro.

1) It has a beginning, middle and end.

2) It is happening in the moment, though in a dream.

3) It is just between the two people.

4) It is life or death of a relationship, because of the physical death.

5) It is founded in a familial love.

6) It is three minutes or under.

Dramedy—Irony in death, then new life of a relationship.

FOREVER

By Peter DeAnello

What? Where? What are *you* doing here? You shouldn't be here! Because, I drove into that car, doing eighty miles-per-hour, to get away from you. What were you doing in someone else's car? Asphyxiation. I thought about carbon monoxide too, but I figured it would take too long. No kidding? We both finally did it this time, huh? What timing? Dumb luck!

So, where is this place? Where is everyone, like spirits, old pets and stuff? Wait a minute? Which place is this? It must be, it has to be, because I left the other place to get away from you, and now…I guess, "for better or worse" is an understatement, huh?

But, you look good, you know? You're younger and *in shape*. You're right, my pants fit again. It's been a long time since I saw my shoes, huh? And, we're not yelling at each other. There's nothing to throw at me. In fact, there's nothing…anywhere. That's kinda cool…

You know, maybe it's not that other place. I'm feeling things I never thought I could feel again. I mean, I can't take my eyes off you. You're a knockout! You're smiling again, and your eyes sparkle. No scars on your wrists either.

Hear that? It's our wedding song. You know, I would like to dance. Would you sing to me while we dance? You think anyone would notice if later we…(giggling) I'm gonna like this place forever, as long as forever is with you.

1) It has a beginning, middle and end.

2) It is happening in the moment.

3) It is just between the two people.

4) It is the death, then new life of a relationship.

5) It is founded in renewed love.

6) It is three minutes or under.

5

Writing Your Own Monologue With The Six Step Process

THE BENEFITS OF WRITING YOUR OWN MONOLOGUE

It's a wonderful feeling, after you finish an original piece, to have an auditioner say, "Wow, that was great! Who wrote that?"

If you've ever written a short story, poem, book, or script, how did it make you feel when someone appreciated your work? It's a wonderful feeling to be able to step back and say to yourself, "I wrote that."

Again, being emotionally attached to your acting work (as the author) places you in a very good position in the audition process. Also, as I've mentioned before, this added advantage is the reason many university professors discourage self-authored monologues. I appreciate and understand that perfectly for the academic world, however, the monologue has launched careers in Hollywood and professional theatre.

Example? Chazz Palminteri launched his career with his one-man play, *A Bronx Tale,* which he later developed into a film script. That movie became Robert DeNiro's directorial debut.

It all began with a monologue based on Mr. Palminteri's childhood experience.

I had the honor of stage-managing Mr. Palminteri's second play, *Faithful,* in Los Angeles. One of the jewels of knowledge I gained from that experience was the importance of actors launching their own careers through self-authored work. It wasn't until he took control of his destiny (as an actor) by creating his own vehicle (as a writer) that success occurred in his career. Was it an accident? If success occurs when preparedness meets opportunity, then he created that opportunity in a career where personal success often times lies in the hands of others. So, was it smart business or luck? I believe the man created his own luck and I respect him immensely for it.

Another man who influenced both my career and helped Mr. Palminteri with his career is Dan Lauria. Mr. Lauria has been a friend and mentor of mine since we met in New York City in 1982. You know Mr. Lauria as the father from the hit television series, *The Wonder Years.* He encouraged and provided the opportunity for Mr. Palminteri to author his own monologue/one-man show, *A Bronx Tale.* He saw the experience through to an Off Broadway production in New York and finally to the film.

I met Mr. Lauria when I was a young actor, fresh out of my acting apprenticeship.

He helped to lift me up and dust off the wreckage after I failed dismally at producing my own one act play in New York, a play that also began as a monologue.

That showcase production was not a financial success for me, but the cherished mentorship and friendship that developed from it has lasted for years.

He has encouraged many actors to self-author vehicles for auditions and production. Because of his encouragement and advice, Dan Lauria is personally responsible for so many success stories in Los Angeles and professional theatre today. That was my experience, however; the moral of the story is that by writing my own vehicle, a lasting friendship and business relationship was created.

WHY NOT TAKE ADVANTAGE OF IT?

I mentioned earlier how many of the opportunities and career-building decisions of this business lie in the hands of others. If you've spent any significant amount of time building a career in theatre, television or the motion picture industry, the last statement rings very true, doesn't it?

Consider that in most professional careers (physician, attorney, accountant, sales management, computer, software, dental, etc., etc., etc.), the amount of work put into study and proper education (though not a guarantee) helps to insure notoriety and financial success in the professional-business world.

That idea, that belief, that fact is not necessarily applicable to a career in show business. Acting is such a subjective business.

However, you can help to create security *when preparedness meets opportunity.*

Preparedness is making sure you are ready with sharpened tools for every audition experience.

In Hollywood, as well as professional theatre, original (un-produced) works are not only more welcome than revival scripts, they are starved for. Just pick up a copy of the Dramatists Guild's Newsletter and check all the new play contests out there each year.

Back to the monologue…

There are biographies of respected actors that are filled with stories of how careers were made with the right audition material. Heading that list is the monologue.

THE MYTH CONCERNING STRUCTURE

Whether you want to write for yourself or to share your work with others, understand that good writing begins with good structure. The Six Steps are the structural foundation for a successful monologue.

Steve Klayman is one of my best friends. He is also an accomplished Hollywood screenwriter, producer and director. When I started writing screenplays, he would read them and offer the same note each time. He would patiently say, "Peter, you are a creative guy, but your scripts lack story structure."

I always argued that I didn't want to be confined, or limited by structure. I was, after all, *an artist* and needed to be unencumbered by limitations.

Malarkey! When I was offered my first paid job as a screenwriter and had to deliver the script in a month, I pleaded with Steve to help me with story structure. He did and I spent the next few days establishing a solid foundation for the story.

Lo and behold, in three and a half weeks, I handed in a script that the producer was very pleased with. It possessed a rising level of conflict in a structurally clear, gripping story line. The script not only worked but I had so much fun because the structure freed me to enjoy the process and just create.

IRONY AT ITS BEST

I thought structure in writing would limit and confine me, but it freed me to be more creative within an understandable and specific world.

I've structured every story since then, from monologue to screenplay. Now, I teach structure as a necessity when writing any script.

We all need a map to get where we're going. Why would it be different in writing? We're taking the audience on a journey, aren't we? It's only fair that we lead them to the destination without abandoning them on the road somewhere. We also don't want them to abandon the journey because of confusion along the way.

So, there is a simple structure in writing your own monologue. Trust that it will free you to be the creative artist you always aspire to be.

Following the Six Step Process, let's begin the process of writing your monologue.

*IMPORTANT:

The order of the Six Steps changes a little here, because we're now approaching the piece as a writer.

For example, when we are *reading* another author's monologue, I ask you to first consider whether it has a beginning, middle and end. In the *writing* of the piece, that is the last step. So, don't get confused, just follow me.

1) BEGIN WITH A LIFE OR DEATH SITUATION

This is where all good monologues begin. If your monologue is not founded in a situation of extreme life or death, your piece won't ever reach its full emotional potential.

All well-written stories occur at the height of conflict. We have a protagonist (the hero of the story) who has to overcome some impossible odds, whether internally or externally (preferably both), to achieve a goal.

In a monologue situation, the conflict has to be stated at the beginning. You must present a life or death situation from the beginning. Remember,

1) Life or death of a relationship

2) The threat of physical harm

3) Life or death of an emotion

So, here is where you start. What's threatening our protagonist? Is he or she,

1) being held at gunpoint?

2) discovering that his/her spouse is cheating, leaving, dying?

3) confronting a loved one for one last and final time to settle something? Is there a risk that he/she will pull that love away if an understanding is not reached?

Remember this very important story tip:

Your protagonist can only be as powerful and righteous as the forces of evil against him/her are threatening and dangerous.

For example, Superman, James Bond and Batman do not ultimately battle the small-time thief, they battle the evil force that wants to take over the world (or a significant part of it).

Meaning, if the situation is not life or death and at the height of conflict, the audience is sleeping instead of on the edge of their seats. It's the same for a monologue.

In the monologue, your *hook* actively defines the life or death situation at hand.

Every story needs a *hook*. It's that initial moment where you either pique an interest in the auditioner or lose him/her if it isn't strong enough, or non-existent.

At the very core of what you do in acting is to take action toward a goal. The very first thing most actors do when they pick up a script is to begin learning the dialogue.

My first question to an actor when they read over a monologue for the first time is, "What are you doing?"

Notice that I didn't ask, "What is *the character* doing?" *You are* the character, so start speaking in those terms from the beginning.

The secret to *hooking* your audience is exposing the life or death situation through *action* and not just declaring it with words.

Just spouting out exposition sounds something like this:

> Jimmy, we've been married for three years. I'm standing in front of the door and you want to leave.

Hooking, with action is stated more like this:

> Jimmy, if you want to leave that bad, you're going to have to pry me away from this door. There's no way I'm letting you walk out on three years of marriage without a fight!

Which set-up causes you to inch toward the edge of your seat?

So, *hooking* the audience *with action* is a matter of beginning the monologue at the ensuing height of conflict, instead of just spouting out exposition to set up the scene for the audience.

Through the second example, *we immediately* know that there's going to be a showdown over the life or death of a relationship.

Notice that the second hook was also *founded in love*.

In a monologue this happens within the first five seconds of the piece. File what I'm about to say as one of the most important lessons in acting…

It's what you *do* that becomes more important than what you *say*.

I tell all new writers to make your characters speak when they *have to*.

2) ONLY CONFRONT ONE PERSON

Keep everyone else out of the equation. Keep the conflict and action just between two people. Remember, a third party adds confusion to the auditioner (audience). We don't know that third person, so the auditioner has to work harder to understand the back-story to your piece. Keep them *in the moment* by keeping the conflict specifically between just you and the person you are confronting.

3) FOUNDED IN LOVE

Can we relate to a person who is making one last ditch effort to save a marriage? Whether married or not, we should know what's it's like to defend someone or something because we care.

Every story needs to be founded in love.

But, what about a life or death situation, where the person holding a gun on you is a killer?

Do you love yourself? How much? What do you have to live for?

Can we all relate to that? If a person stands in front of a loaded gun and responds with "Go ahead, I'm a born loser anyway," who cares? If he doesn't care, why should we?

If that person starts to sweat and the blood rushes to his feet, can we relate? Have you ever been afraid of someone or something?

Remember always that love is the strongest emotion to work from. Hate, fear, anger, hurt, etc. are all derived from *love*.

4) THE MOMENT OF TRUTH—THE TICKING CLOCK. WHY NOW AND ONLY NOW?

One of the most important points in this process is to define clearly why this event can only occur at *this time*?

If the confrontation can happen at any time, the stakes are not high enough. This creates *the ticking clock* (the moment of truth) that drives the best stories.

I find myself in workshops, asking over and over again, "why now?" For example, if you return home to find your husband walking out the door, bags packed, the meter running in the taxi, all due to your infidelity, when is the only time available to fight to keep him? Now and only now. That is the defining moment of the relationship, the moment of truth.

But, if you walk into the study when he's working and ask him if it's a good time to talk, we're not on the edge of our seats. We may watch your acting technique and appreciate your work, but we're not at the edge of our seats. Does that make sense?

Why must your monologue's life or death situation occur now and only now? You must answer that before you continue, or you will cripple the process.

Remember, "I remember when..." and "Once upon a time..." (the story approach) monologues don't work well. They take the auditioner out of the action of the piece, and you make that person a spectator to (not involved in) your work. Again, the auditioner is a spectator to some extent, but go back to asking yourself, "What puts me at the edge of my seat when watching a good movie or play?"

If you (as an audience member) can relate to the emotional struggle of the character at that moment, then the writer, director and actors are in the driver's seat.

WHO, WHAT, WHEN, WHERE, WHY AND HOW?

Complete your outline with these questions:

A) Who am I talking to? Evaluate, in depth, your relationship with this person, and make the stakes as high as possible. Since, in the Six Step Process, you are talking to just one person to settle a conflict, that person needs to be the most important person in your life at this point in time. Clearly define your relationship in detail.

B) What do I want from this person? Every actor has asked the question, "What is my objective?" Again, the stakes have to be as high as you can possibly imagine. Every protagonist in a story wants something from another person to achieve a goal. What is it and how does it directly relate to the person you are confronting, or the person confronting you?

C) Where is this confrontation occurring?

1) Where physically?

2) Where in your life, in terms of your inner growth, or in your relationship with the other person?

D) When is it taking place?

1) What time of day, and how is that relevant to the story and its possible outcomes?

2) When in this person's life? Did he/she just get out of rehab? Was there an accident of some kind? A life-changing event?

E) Why?

1) Why must this conflict only occur at this time?

2) Why here, physically, mentally or emotionally?

F) How is it occurring? Here, many times, is where the irony is written into the story.

Example;

If you've seen the original *Lethal Weapon* film, Mel Gibson's character approaches a man about to jump from a rooftop and commit suicide. His job, as a police officer, is to talk the distraught man down from jumping. Instead, he climbs out on the edge of the roof with him. What this distraught man doesn't know is that Mr. Gibson's character is more suicidal than he is at this moment in time.

That's Irony.

So, instead of coaxing him down the way he is supposed to, he challenges the man to jump with him. When the man hesitates, Mr. Gibson's character realizes that man didn't want to jump in the first place. Mr. Gibson then grabs the man by the hand and jumps, pulling them both down into a large police balloon. As Mr. Gibson rolls off the balloon onto the ground, the distraught man is heard yelling, "He's crazy!" That is irony based on *how*.

REMEMBER—ASKING YOURSELF "WHAT IF?" CREATES IRONY

IRONY—

This topic needs to be discussed and understood, because it is such a pivotal structural tool, used in every great script. It can occur, not only through answering the *how* question, but with all the others as well.

The best way to seek out irony is to set up your situation, fill in the blanks of the character description, then ask yourself, "What if."

At some point during the writing of *Lethal Weapon,* Shane Black set up the jumper and asked himself, "What if the police officer trying to help the jumper wants to commit suicide more than the jumper does?"

See how that happens?

Here's a life or death situation:

A man enters his home and finds his wife cheating on him. He confronts her by putting a gun to her head. *What if* she's feeling so guilty that she pulls out her own gun and puts it to her own head? The husband then lowers his gun and begs her not to shoot herself.

"What if?" Is the most important question you can ask yourself to create irony.

So, let's write that piece together, but before we start,

5) THINK THREE MINUTES OR UNDER

You have permission to rewrite every piece you author. In fact, it was Mario Puzo who stated, "The art of writing is rewriting."

That quote was pasted over my computer for many years as a reminder to myself.

Very seldom will any good writer present the first draft of anything as a finished work. It can always be better.

So, go ahead and over-write the first draft. Just make sure you edit it down under three minutes for presentation as a monologue. *Leave them wanting more* is the general rule. Also, remember that your auditioner will usually reach a conclusion regarding your talent within the first minute (usually within the first ten to fifteen seconds).

6) A COMPLETE WORK

Remember not to leave your auditioner unfulfilled.

You may leave your audience with a question, but don't cut the story short just to fulfill the three minute rule.

Let's write a monologue

Return to the life or death situation. Let's start the monologue in the middle of the life or death of a relationship, as the husband has already found his wife cheating.

It is not important to acknowledge who the lover is, or else we would have to introduce another character. The identity of the lover is not as important as the wife's infidelity.

Now, let's present the first *what if? What if* he was searching for his gun as they confront her infidelity? He *hooks* the audience in the midst of action, by asking a question.

PAY BACK

By Peter DeAnello

What do you think I'm doing? Looking for my pistol! I told you if you ever cheated on me, I was going to shoot you. So where is it?

Now, *what if* she produces the pistol and points it at her own head? That creates the first *irony*.

What are you doing? Put that down. Don't play with that, it might go off! C'mon, you can get hurt, cut it out. Look, nothing's worth shooting yourself over. I wasn't really going to shoot you. You know that. I was just going to scare you so you won't ever cheat on me again. C'mon, tell me you're sorry and give it to me. Say something. Put the safety back on, baby. C'mon, let's be honest, I deserve it. I know that's the only reason you did it.

Here's the second bit of irony. She cheated on him and he's offering the explanation for why she did it (instead of her). He admits that he deserved it. In essence, she cheated on him and he's the one confessing.

It's about pay back. Alright, fine, truce, OK? I'll stop...OK? Now, take it out of your mouth. OK, I promise, no more finding panties under the bed. No more late nights at the office. Are you happy? (Still no response) What do you want from me? Say something! OK, fine, you want me to go for it all...No more trips without you...And, I'll get rid of the hotel key. (Still nothing) Hey, Saint Michael, I'm not! (Still no response) I've got nothing left to confess here! (Still nothing). Fine, you've got your second honeymoon. I'll pick up the tickets today. We'll go next month. OK, you big baby?

No more of this for either one of us. We'll put our rings back on and start over. Deal? (He sighs as she takes the gun from her mouth) Good, put the safety on.

Isn't this a barrel of laughs? You cheat on me and I feel like I just left the confessional. I feel better, you know? This is a good thing...Cleansing and all...Releasing...Cleaning out the conscience, like a good enema or something.

But, if you do it again, I'll kill you. Now, let's put our rings on and call the travel agent.

1) It has a beginning, middle and end.

2) It is happening in the moment.

3) It is just between the two people. It would have been easy to involve a third person, but that would have detracted from the piece.

4) It is life or death of a relationship and the threat of physical death.

5) It is founded in love.

6) It is three minutes or under.

The best monologues contain life or death of a relationship *and* the threat of physical death.

It makes sense that when the stakes are at their highest, the monologue is at its most exciting and interesting.

Now, let's write a second piece:
Create the life or death situation

Let's look for an idea that *physically embraces* the *ticking clock* situation.

What if we used a *stopwatch* to literally create the ticking clock?

Now, *what if* the stopwatch represented the amount of time someone had to offer a confession?

What if we choose the threat of *physical death*? Let's offer a verbal *ultimatum* to support the ticking clock device.

What if the confessor is a thief?

What if we describe the worst tortures one could imagine? (Again, the stakes need to be at their highest)

Since this scenario reeks of a *hit man* situation, why not embrace it as so, *tough guy* and all. We first need an *active* statement that *hooks,* as well as informs, our audience.

TOUGH GUY

By Peter DeAnello

Don't make me the bad guy here, Georgie. I love you like a son and this is the way you pay me back? I've gotta make things ugly, but I ain't the guy who stole, right? Somebody's gotta pay and all fingers are pointing in your direction.

Who's the thief here? You've gotta admit it and break my heart, Georgie. But, if that's the way it is, then that's what I gotta live with it. Just don't make me live the rest of my life knowin you're a thief *and* a liar.

So, I want you to really think about this before I make you hit the button on that stopwatch. Once you do, you've got thirty seconds to do the right thing...half a minute to ease your punishment. I always make the guilty party hit the button. Why? So after the torture is over, I can walk away knowing *you* did what's coming to *yourself.* I need *three words* to change the direction of things.

What if Georgie refuses to talk through the thirty-second count down? This will create more anticipation and anxiety.

What if we create even more anxiety by having the actor describe the worst tortures imaginable during that time?

Hey, wait a minute? Didn't I skip a step or two? No. You'll discover the answers to the questions, w*ho, what, when, where, how and where's the love* in a moment.

Now, is there anything you want to tell me, tough guy? The stone faced routine, huh? OK, fine. You think I haven't dealt with this before? You think you're the first guy to challenge me? Twenty-five seconds!

I guarantee every tough guy cries when the moment of truth comes. When you're starin into two barrels, when you're hanging twenty stories, when you're sinking to the bottom of the sea...Twenty seconds! When the noose tightens around your neck, when the dirt is bein shoveled over you, when the last thing you remember is your heart beatin so hard and fast, you swear it's gonna bust out of your chest...Ten seconds...When you're so scared you can't remember your name...When you're about to enter the next world and you don't know what's scarier, leavin this one or enterin that one, cause it's the fact that you're a bad guy that got you in this predicament in the first place! Three, two...

What if Georgie now confesses?
What if Georgie is just eight years old?
What if Georgie only stole a meatball sandwich?

(He relaxes) "I did it." Those are the three words, Georgie. Why did you make me have to be the bad guy here? Why couldn't you save me the nervous time here? I just wanna know one thing before we forget this…was it good? Not the confession, the meatball sandwich? Of course it was, cause *I* made it, the way *I* like it. Steal my meatball hero again and I'll really get mad next time. Your punishment? What do you think? I'm not gonna be easy on you. I'm gonna make another meatball sandwich, *bigger* than the one you stole, and eat it *right in front of you*! See? Now you cry. What'd I tell ya? No more tough guy now, huh? I told you I'd make you pay big.

Alright, alright, I'll share it with you, just stop crying, but then you gotta go to bed. What are you gonna do when you turn nine, steal my pasta maker? Now, give me a kiss and say you're sorry…tough guy.

    1) It has a beginning, middle and end.

    2) It is happening in the moment.

    3) It is talking to just one person.

    4) It is the threat of physical death.

    5) It is founded in love.

    6) It is three minutes or under.

Can you describe the ironies in this piece? Think about what takes this piece from drama to comedy. Remember that irony is comedy's best ally.

Let's write one more:

What's the life or death struggle? A popular topic is drugs, but let's look for another angle on that, instead of what's always already been done.

If our character overdoses, it creates the ticking clock in a *life or death situation*. But *what if* he/she does it on purpose? Let's keep this piece genderless.

What if our protagonist tries to steal from a loved one, but instead of seeking money for drugs, he/she steals just to see if the person will be willing to enable that habit?

In most cases, it's the person who isn't on drugs that is the strongest one in the scene. *What if* the strong person is the drug addict this time and the weak person is the enabler (the person who surrenders over the money as a means of protecting the drug addict from getting caught or to keep that person's love).

What if the enabler is the drug addict's mother?

Let's make it a Drama.

RUSSIAN ROULETTE

By Peter DeAnello

I don't think a gun will stop me. Then again, it depends on where you shoot me, doesn't it? I probably won't feel it anyway, so knock yourself out. You're the one that thought it would be a good idea to try new things. So, coke led to heroin, etcetera, etcetera, and etcetera.

Hey, how many bullets do you have in that gun? Is there one for my brain, because it hurts, right down to my stomach, what's left of it. So, if you're not going to shoot me, I need money. Where else would I go? Give me something to sell! Anything. What do you mean, "there's nothing left?" What kind of crap is that? (a long beat)

Good for you, Mom. You passed the first test. I don't want to hurt you anymore. That's really why I'm here. When your own mother pulls a gun on you, things get more serious, don't they? I can appreciate that.

So, here we are in the writing, at the moment of truth, when the protagonist (main character, good guy) turns the tables on the person who is the antagonist (the enabler). We've also changed the story from the typical, "I'm on drugs and need money" story by asking *what if?*

1) We have created a life or death situation.

2) We've stayed accountable to the rule of talking *to just one person.*

3) If the drug addict comes to the mother out of tough love for her, and begs her for tough love in return, then it is *founded in love*, but with a twist.

(A long beat) Don't cry…Because, I've got good news…I did what you couldn't, because you're weak. Look at me! If you love me, then make the call. Who? Call an ambulance, the hospital, and the law. Your kid is a criminal. In my last moment of sanity, I OD'd and called an ambulance cause if I make it through, I'll be a ward of the state and presto, I'll get *help*.

4) What keeps it in the moment is the overdose. It *can't happen at any other time*.

I'm an addict and you've been in denial. You choose a gun? You have the power to commit me and you choose a gun? What the hell kind of love is that? It's weak, that's what it is. Toughen up. You're all I have and I need *tough*. I need *mega-tough*. Cause Mom, you can't let me get away with this anymore. It's not fair to *you* and it's not fair to *me*. So, now I'm playing Russian Roulette with an ambulance.

5) We'll keep this **three minutes or under** by getting to the point and add-ing the ticking clock of the ambulance and overdose.

6) Remember, we can give it **a beginning, middle and end**, but still leave the clock ticking. That's how you keep the audience on the edge of their seats, wanting more, and still fulfill the story.

(Dizzy) I love you, Mom, but if I make it through this and ever get hooked again, don't be so weak. Hold me, and if I wake up, slap me.

Ending the piece with "slap me" fortifies the idea of tough love.

CONCLUSION

Congratulations! You now have a new and complete understanding on the mysteries surrounding the need for, use of, and proper foundation of the monologue. I've outlined just what makes the monologue a success tool in building acting careers.

Confidence, in any procedure or product, builds when information is absorbed and turned into practice. Remember, when information is low, fear (due to the unknown) is high. When information is absorbed, fear diminishes.

Both the independent contractor and the artist in you now possess the useful and creative tools to insure that your craft is nurtured and presented in the most successful way possible.

Please allow me to suggest again that you read this book twice. First to understand the material and its application, and second to implement the Six Steps (either in your search for winning monologues, or as a template in writing your own).

I've outlined how structure frees, rather than inhibits, the artist. I encourage you to embrace structure in art, especially in the writing and acting process.

Here are the confidence building benefits you are now able to employ in your chosen business and art. Allow this book to be an insurance policy in several areas of approach and application:

1) **Valuable audition tips**. If an insurance policy existed for actors to cover all the right business practices in the audition process, it would include the tips outlined in this book. You now have them, so put them into practice. Remember that just because a habit feels comfortable, it may not be your most successful or professional choice. Give yourself the credit and opportunity you deserve by putting to use the most successful audition habits.

2) **A clearer picture means no wasted time.** Now, as you sift through the infinite libraries of scripts and monologue books, you have a template for

quickly locating and easily recognizing those structurally sound monologues that best showcase your talent. That means no more wasted time in the searching process. Anyone, in any situation, will become discouraged when the mountain seems too high to climb.

3) Collaborative effort. For the first time, you (as the actor) have a *confidence gauge* to insure that the writer's work is on an equally creative level in the audition process. Use the Six Step Process to determine whether your presentation is handicapped from the start, or has every opportunity to be a success in each audition.

4) Artistically powerful. You now have the best opportunity to successfully own the only part of the audition process that is truly in your control, your auditioner's *emotional attachment to your work*. Engage and grip your auditioner/audience by allowing them to become involved in your work.

5) Tools to write your own success vehicle. The Six Steps are now your tools to create an artistic blueprint for easily constructing a dynamic, self-authored monologue. I love the Nike ad on television. They've coined the phrase, *Just Do It.* Here's your opportunity to embrace those three words that will prove to the artist in you that:

a. there's an easier way to locate a dynamic monologue

b. you have more control over your career in the audition process, both as an actor and a writer.

6) Monologues to use. You have 50 original monologues, most genderless, to audition with or to use as a template to create your own.

FOR ACADEMIC ORGANIZATIONS

I hope this book will arouse a need as well as a place for the self-authored monologue within the academic world. While it is important for young actors to realize that most of their experience will be gained through the writing of already published authors, I also encourage a need for the student actor to have a template for locating, as well as authoring, audition material. Hopefully, together, we can encourage and develop young actors and writers in the process, as well as offer them another option for control in a career that lies so much in the hands of others.

WORKSHOP SEMINARS AND CONTACT INFORMATION

Peter DeAnello offers workshop seminars for schools, universities, and independent organizations. Mr. DeAnello's seminars include:

Write To Act—The Monologue To The Scene

Write To Act—The Playwriting and Screenwriting Process

Own The Audition, Book The Job
The Actor's Eight Point Process for Script Breakdown and Character Development

Motivation For The Actor

If you would like more information concerning the workshops offered by Mr. DeAnello, please contact him at:

Peter DeAnello
Actorwriter.Com &
Write To Act Workshop Seminars
PO Box 189
Broomfield, CO 80038-0189

Or through www.actorwriter.com

0-595-30918-6

Made in the USA
Lexington, KY
26 April 2010